ON THE WATCHTOWER
A HISTORY OF FIRE LOOKOUTS

ON THE WATCHTOWER
A HISTORY OF FIRE LOOKOUTS

DIXIE BOYLE

SUNSTONE PRESS
SANTA FE

© 2025 by Dixie Boyle
All Rights Reserved
No part of this book may be reproduced in any form or by any electronic or mechanical means including
information storage and retrieval systems without permission in writing from the publisher, except by a reviewer who may quote brief passages in a review.
Sunstone books may be purchased for educational, business, or sales promotional use.
For information please write: Special Markets Department, Sunstone Press, P.O. Box 2321, Santa Fe, New Mexico 87504-2321.
Printed on acid-free paper
∞
ebook: 978-1-61139-784-0

Library of Congress Cataloging-in-Publication Data

Names: Boyle, Dixie author
Title: On the watchtower : a history of fire lookouts / Dixie Boyle.
Description: Santa Fe : Sunstone Press, [2025] | Summary: "A History of Fire Lookouts and their vanishing history"-- Provided by publisher.
Identifiers: LCCN 2025051375 | ISBN 9781632937742 paperback | ISBN 9781611397840 epub
Subjects: LCSH: Fire lookouts--West (U.S.) | Women fire lookouts--West (U.S.) | Fire lookout stations--West (U.S.) | Forest fires--Detection
Classification: LCC SD421.375 .B69 2026 | DDC 634.96180978--dc23/eng/20251209
LC record available at https://lccn.loc.gov/2025051375

WWW.SUNSTONEPRESS.COM
SUNSTONE PRESS / POST OFFICE BOX 2321 / SANTA FE, NM 87504-2321 /USA
(505) 988-4418

APPRECIATION AND ACKNOWLEDGMENT OF THE LADY FIRE LOOKOUTS

I want to show appreciation and acknowledge the early lady fire lookouts who paved the way for other women to be able to work in the field. When the U.S. Forest Service began to establish fire lookouts in the early years of the 20th Century, women were not considered for the primary lookout positions. Government officials felt women could not handle the physical requirements of the job nor live in a wilderness setting on their own for an entire fire season.

Over a decade would pass before northern California's Klamath National Forest hired the first woman to officially staff a fire lookout for the U.S. Forest Service in 1913. Hallie Daggett made newspaper headlines when she accepted Eddy Gulch Fire Lookout. She was the perfect woman to open the way for other women to serve as fire lookouts. She loved the outdoors, was familiar with the territory, enjoyed the isolation and more importantly was well respected as a fire lookout by the public as well as her superiors.

Hallie reported forty fires her first season pinpointing them all when they were small and establishing her reputation as a fire lookout. She seldom asked for help and cut and stacked her own firewood plus early in the season gathered snow with a shovel to melt for her drinking water. She was paid $840.00 for the entire fire season and received two days off a month, if she was lucky.

She often dressed as a wilderness ranger or wore ankle-length skirts. She started strapping a revolver to her belt after seeing a panther near the lookout one evening. She was independent, capable and not afraid to live on the mountain alone for months at a time.

Hallie retired in 1927 from lookout duty. In the 1950s residents of her home town in Etna, California built her a log cabin on Main Street next to the home of her sister. She lived in the cabin until her death in 1964. Later, the cabin was donated to the City of Etna in 1993 for a park and historic site.

Hallie Daggett, the first woman to officially staff a fire lookout.
(Courtesy of U.S. Forest Service)

Five years after Hallie was hired to staff Eddy Gulch, Alice Henderson was hired to staff Mt. Kineo Fire Lookout near Moosehead Lake in Maine. Since she began her new job in 1918, she became the second woman to officially staff a fire lookout.

Alice Henderson of Gardiner, Maine is credited with being the first lady fire lookout in New England. She was offered work at Mt. Kineo Fire Lookout near Moosehead Lake. She had the perfect credentials for the position, as she had spent the two previous summers working in sporting camps in the area. She knew the territory well, and was said to be a lover of the woods and nature.

Not only did Alice have to pack in her supplies for the lookout, but she was responsible to maintain two and a half miles of phone line to the lookout tower. When not looking for fires, she often worked on knitting for the Red Cross.

In newspaper interviews, Alice stated that she found her life on the lookout tower very interesting and she was seldom bored. She related that she had only two fires since she was hired to staff the lookout and sighted another over the border in Canada. When it rained she could leave the lookout tower and head to civilization to pick up more supplies. She carried most of the things she bought about twelve pounds worth, which she packed in her knapsack, strapped on her back and climbed up a mountain trail near three miles long.

Newspaper headlines of the era touted Henderson's position as one of the curious war-time occupations of women. She was considered brave and many were interested in her occupation. She often received between 20 and 30 visitors each day when the weather was good.

As many lady lookouts she was not afraid to be alone and made pets or acquaintances out of the wild animals near the tower. She befriended a hedgehog, owls, squirrels, a special deer or two and even a cow moose.

Alice Henderson, first lady lookout in New England circa 1918. (Courtesy Rachel Frith)

Two more women were hired to staff fire lookouts the following year in 1919. One from Colorado's Pike National Forest the other from New Mexico's Zuni Mountains. Helen Dowe, a former newspaper reporter and artist, spent three fire seasons staffing Devil's Head Fire Lookout near Denver.

The *Denver Post* dated September 19, 1920, told about the influence Helen had on other women throughout the country wanting to work as a fire lookout, "The success she has attained as the first woman fire lookout, and the widespread publicity she has received in magazines and motion pictures has led thousands of girls throughout the country to make applications for similar positions." Helen received thousands of letters from women wanting to know about the life of a fire lookout and how they could land a position.

Helen Dow, early fire lookout in Colorado. (Courtesy U.S. Forest Service)

After three years at Devil's Head, Helen decided to work on a U.S. Forest Service surveying crew and became the first woman in the country to do so. But, more significantly she is credited with inspiring hundreds of women to apply for jobs as fire lookouts throughout the nation.

Lucy Whiteside at her Café with western actors Dub Taylor and Tex Harding.
(Courtesy Mary Alice Hinsinger)

The next female lookout has not received as much publicity as Helen, but also in 1919 Lucy Whiteside of New Mexico's Cibola National Forest served as the primary lookout on Mt. Sedgwick. She was offered the job after her husband who had the position was murdered by a neighbor in 1918. The Whitesides were the first lookouts to staff the lookout site.

The Whiteside Ranch was at the base of Mt. Sedgwick making it convenient to staff the lookout and look after the ranch at the same time. An article in the *Carrizozo Outlook* in November of 1920 tells about her skills as a lookout and firefighter, "Lucy has considerable experience fighting fires both during the time that her husband was fire guard and later, and has successfully fought more than one fire single handed."

Lucy Whiteside was the first woman in New Mexico to staff a fire lookout between 1919 and 1920. But she would move on to be better known as Mother Whiteside a midwife and café and hotel owner along historic, Route 66. She is credited with delivering 500 babies in the Grants area and often gave away food at her café to those in need

Many described her business as an oasis in the desert between Albuquerque and Gallup. Those who frequented her establishment knew she always had a pot of coffee on, and if she had gone to bed there was a roast in the oven. Her customers were asked to leave the correct change on the dining room sideboard. She was loved and respected by the community and the local library was dedicated to her.

With the onslaught of World War II, many lookout posts were left vacant throughout the country as men were needed in the war effort. For the first time, this gave women more opportunities to serve as the primary fire lookout. Although government officials as well as the American public were still skeptical of women staffing fire lookouts on their own, this did not stop them from applying for the position.

On South Dakota's Black Hills National Forest, Minnie Cooper was one of the first women to staff a fire tower when she accepted work on Elk Mountain near the Wyoming border in 1943. Minnie was quite the pioneer and instantly took to the life of a fire lookout.

It is not uncommon for these lady lookouts to spend decades on their mountain peaks. Virginia or Ginny Vincent, a lookout in Montana's Lolo National Forest, staffed Stark Mountain Lookout west of Missoula for 39 fire seasons making her one of the nation's longest working fire lookouts. She was known throughout the region for her accuracy in reporting wildfire and for her love of nature.

Ginny received a degree in Zoology from the University of Vermont and worked at Cornell and Princeton Universities before moving to Montana. She loved nature and knew all the plants and birds. She often gave nature tours and documented the plants in the area.

Ginny first thought about becoming a fire lookout after reading an article on lookouts while a teenager living in New Jersey. She applied for a lookout job in 1960, but during this era in fire management the person hired as the lookout also had to extinguish the blaze they spotted and maintain phone lines to the lookout site.

Since she was a woman, she was not considered for the job. She tried again in 1970 and this time landed Stark Mountain Lookout beating out two men who had also applied for the position. The lookout site became her summer home and vocation for almost four decades until she was in her eighties. She was an extremely dedicated fire lookout and fortunately her contributions have been documented by the U.S. Forest Service.

Martha Hardy worked as a fire lookout at Tatoosh Fire Lookout in the Cascades of Washington State. She made friends with chipmunks and squirrels and seemed to enjoy the lookout life. She worked the lookout for one season in 1946 and had to repair downed phone lines as well as haul her own water. But, she like other women in the field proved women could also handle the job as a fire lookout.

Martha published a book about her experiences on the lookout with the one-word title of Tatoosh the name of her lookout tower. The book was an immediate success upon its publication and has been reprinted several times. Martha would go on to publish another book named Skyo. After staffing the lookout, she bought a small ranch and old cabin in the area and lived there part of the year. In this book she writes about the City of Packwood and the Cowlitz Valley.

Martha gives delightful descriptions of lookout life in her book. In those days many of the lookout sites were extremely isolated and when the lookout accepted the position knew they would be on their own for most of the summer. The lookout was often packed in with their food and supplies hoping they would last until another pack string could make it to the lookout tower. Martha described the pack string getting ready to take her to her new summer home, "The pack string was about a city block down the side of the peak, rickracking through the drifts."

Martha loved lookout life and was an exceptional lookout. She was not afraid of the wilderness and often embraced lookout life. She told others about her experiences and did many lectures about lookout life after her summer as a fire lookout.

Martha spent one season as a fire lookout and worked as a high school math teacher and later as a professor of mathematics at the University of Washington in Seattle. Martha enjoyed giving talks about her lookout experience over the years. She passed away in 1999 at the age of 81.

In conclusion, I want to acknowledge one last lady lookout my long-time lookout partner Linda Powell who served on Gallinas Fire Lookout in the Cibola National Forest for three decades. We worked together for over twenty years, endured many a long and intense fire season, always had one another's backs, triangulated multiple fires over the years and were good friends from the first day we met. She was the perfect partner, and there will never be another one like her.

For fifteen years or so the Cibola National Forest had a core of fire lookouts who returned to their lookout stations each year. The group got together in the off season and helped one another during fire season. As members of the group started to retire or pass away, it was bittersweet to see them go, and I missed hearing their voices on the radio. Linda's retirement has affected me the most, but we all have to make the tough decision of leaving our lookout stations one day.

Linda was an extremely dedicated fire lookout. She pinpointed the fires she reported down to the quarter section of the quarter section, led crews into the fires in a short time, was always helpful and polite on the radio and never missed a fire. It will be hard for the U.S. Forest Service to find another lookout as good as Linda.

Linda Powell served as the Gallinas Fire Lookout for thirty-two years. (Courtesy Gabe Lyons)

I will miss you my dear friend and fire season will not be the same without you. I will always treasure all the years we spent together spotting fires, watching weather patterns, laughing at the antics of the engine crews, relating our wildlife encounters, watching sunsets and sharing the life of a fire lookout.

Currently, the U.S. Forest Service hires as many women as men to staff their fire lookout sites. Women are now accepted as members of engine, hot shot and helitack crews. They serve on fire management teams, hold supervisory positions and even head our national forests. It is hard to imagine, the struggle these early lady fire lookouts endured in order to be able to staff a fire lookout for the U.S. Forest Service and other agencies. Thank you ladies for your dedication and service.

CONTENTS

Preface ~ 19

1 / History of Fire Lookouts in New Mexico ~ 25

2 / History of Fire Lookouts in the Black Hills of Wyoming & South Dakota ~ 75

3 / Lookouts in the Plains States ~ 173

4 / Three Former Lookouts in California ~ 181

Conclusion ~ 187

References ~ 191

Author Biography ~ 195

PREFACE

The lookout life has always appealed to me. Mountains and learning the names of landmarks have been an interest since childhood. While growing up in central New Mexico, I often drove to the top of the Manzano Mountains to visit the fire lookout on Capilla Peak. The lookout was perched up in the clouds and miles from human habitation. The views of the Estancia Valley to the east and the Rio Grande Valley to the west were more than breathtaking. I thought working in a fire lookout would be the perfect job. Communing with nature and watching weather patterns sounded like a good way to make a living.

It was not until after college when I finally got the chance to work and live in an isolated fire lookout and report forest fires. This new profession, which would soon become all-consuming in my life, started in the Gila National Forest in southwestern New Mexico. The Gila was the perfect place to start my career as a fire lookout, since the lookouts still retain that wilderness atmosphere. I was hooked after that first season and was not happy unless working in a fire lookout somewhere year after year afterwards.

I left New Mexico and moved to eastern Oregon where I saw the Great Basin, Cascade Range and Pacific Ocean for the first time. I was surprised to find the land that touched the Great Basin was a lot like the dry land I had left behind. The summer was windy and dry with several complex fires torching much of the forest bordering the John Day Valley. The season ended in rain and the snows of an early winter.

Afterwards, I worked in the Black Hills of Wyoming and South Dakota. I remained in the spiritual country for over a decade and became intimate with the history of the Sioux and Cheyenne Indians. I became acquainted with the Great Plains of the Dakotas. The Great Plains are wide, open country where you can see for miles and the people always have a handshake and a smile. The hypnotic and endless views give the land a sense of vastness and emptiness I have never seen anywhere else.

I drifted back to New Mexico and worked in the Zuni Mountains in the shadow of Mt. Taylor, the ancient volcano worshipped by the Pueblo Indians. The trails, pueblo ruins and artifacts left behind by the Pueblo Indians are in evidence throughout the sacred landscape. Descendants of the first settlers remain.

The Zuni Mountains remain sacred to the Zuni people who continue to hold ceremonies in the mountains and teach their children the stories taught by their ancestors. The land has endured change over the years due to drought, logging, ranching, mining and other signs of progress. Yet, the sacred feeling of the mountains has remained.

I returned to the Black Hills after my summer in the sacred mountains of western New Mexico and remained on the Great Plains for another four years. It was hard to leave the Black Hills, and the peacefulness of the mountains have remained with me ever since. I wish I could have learned more about the people who built and worked on the lookouts. There was always a feeling they were not too far away. The Black Hills was one of the first areas in the west to construct fire lookouts.

Eventually, I returned to the Cibola National Forest in central New Mexico and to the Manzano Mountains of my childhood. The urban interface has encroached on the mountain over the years, but the landmarks have remained the same.

Many people think I am crazy when I tell them I work as a fire lookout. The first questions normally asked are, "What do you do alone all summer? Aren't you bored? To me the job is far from boring, and I truly feel safe on the lookout. Lookouts are required to learn the terrain and be able to interpret the weather. Most of the summer is a peaceful time of watching the skies and wildlife and explaining landmarks to those who visit, but when the lightning starts is when fire season truly begins.

I have had as many as seventeen fires going at one time when I worked on the Elk Mountain District in Newcastle, Wyoming. Other summers I might spot three to five fires. Fire Lookouts are required to report all wildfire to a central dispatch that sends fire equipment and men to the fire as needed. The lookout must pay close attention to the radio traffic and keep crews in the field posted on fires and weather conditions that might affect fire behavior.

Most fire lookouts are in isolated areas with primitive living conditions. The stations normally do not have electricity or running water, and an outhouse serves as the bathroom facilities. In order to spot forest fires, lookout structures stand on the highest peak with the best view. This causes lookout personnel and the structure they inhabit to deal with all types of weather conditions.

I have clocked wind gusts up to 90 mph, had snow on the Fourth of July, been knocked out of my chair by lightning and watched it blow out the repeater and radio. I have seen fire spot (jump) close to half a mile during a hot, windy day in the Zuni Mountains. I have felt winds from a funnel cloud twenty miles in the distance during tornado season in Wyoming. I barely made it off the mountain in four-wheel drive when an unexpected blizzard swept through the Bearlodge Mountains in late September.

More than once, I have had to wait out the rains during monsoon season and float across creeks to make it home. The most heartbreaking was the time I had to watch the winds push flames to the top of the ridge where my lookout sat, while I evacuated to lower and safer ground. A fire lookout encounters all types of weather conditions and needs to be prepared when traveling back and forth to their lookout stations during fire season.

Proponents of the use of cameras in fire lookouts would have the public believe fire lookouts are nearing extinction and their romantic lifestyle will soon belong to the past. Newspaper headlines from New Mexico to Oregon tout the use of cameras over the more traditional use of fire lookouts. Yet, agencies throughout the United States continue to staff close to five hundred fire towers. Many ranger districts have installed cameras in lookouts no longer in use while continuing with personnel for their main fire lookouts.

Advances in technology have made it possible for high-powered cameras, drones and satellite equipment to record and send photos from space plus pinpoint wildfire and other disasters. A GPS, smart phone, computer or other electronic device is most often used when locating a landmark or highway. The world has become a technical society where the majority of the population depends on instant communication.

Lookout personnel equipped with smart phones or the Internet are able to check the radar, track approaching storms and relay information to crews in the field. They can access lightning maps and take photos of fires and send to dispatch centers to help in attacking the blaze. They too can tap into technical devices to help with reporting fires. Yet, in addition to technology they use the Osborne fire finder created over a century earlier in order to pinpoint wildfire down to the quarter section of the quarter section. Are cameras as accurate?

It definitely takes a certain type of an individual to spend weeks and months alone at an isolated fire tower in the wilderness, and long-term lookouts become extremely dedicated and loyal to their lookout stations. It is not uncommon for a lookout to return to their posts for twenty years or more. They know and love the land they over-see and watch the country closely for fire, as most feel it is their responsibility to report fires as quickly and accurately as possible.

Fire Lookouts have a long and distinguished history. Some of the first fire lookouts were stationed overlooking mining camps throughout the West in the 1870s. These camps were often thrown together in a hasty manner with buildings close together, so when a fire started it was hard to stop. A lookout with a pair of binoculars and a bell would hike to the top of the highest peak in the area and glass for fire. If a fire was spotted, the ringing of the lookout's bell alerted everyone to return to camp and help fight the fire.

Two of the earliest lookout points were located above the mining camps of Helena, Montana and Deadwood, South Dakota. The Southern Pacific Railroad built a shelter for a fire lookout near Donner Pass in California's Sierra Nevada Mountains. Soon fire lookouts were popping up on mountain peaks throughout the West in an attempt to keep ahead of the growing fire threat in the mountains where settlers and miners were building homes and moving their families.

Fire towers began to appear on mountain peaks throughout the country and as many as six thousand were once in service. The first lookout personnel found and extinguished the fires they spotted. Corrals were provided at these early lookout stations where the lookout's horse and pack string were kept so they could ride to the fire after reporting it.

At the turn of the twentieth century, fire lookouts or smoke chasers patrolled the newly formed forest reserves on horseback looking for wildfire. They were required to provide their own horse, pack string, tent and enough supplies to last a month. They remained on patrol for a month or more and made sure the different forests were safe from fire and other illegal activities.

These early patrolmen normally followed a route along a high ridge affording a good view. After searching with field glasses at various points along the route, the lookout would camp for the evening and continue his patrol the following day. When a fire was spotted, he would alert crews in the field to the location of the fire. If he could not handle the fire then firefighters were sent in to help with the blaze. Most of the time, the fire patrolman took care of the small fires he encountered.

Most platform and lookout trees were dismantled or sawed down by the 1950s, although trees on high ridges are still utilized by fire fighters looking for wildfire. Next, the wooden towers were replaced with steel ones. Modern lookout towers often possess electricity, fax machines, cell service and provide a place for those staffing the site to sleep, cook and live for five to six months out of the year.

The Civilian Conservation Corps (CCCs) was a relief program enacted by President Franklin D. Roosevelt during the Great Depression. It provided jobs for young, single men during a time when one fourth of the work force was fortunate to be employed. Members of the CCCs lived in the forest and worked on conservation projects and controlling wildfire. With the development of the CCCs came a lookout construction boom not seen before or since. CCC members built and then staffed the fire lookouts they erected. Each lookout station was staffed by two men. When a fire was spotted one man would remain in the lookout for communication while the other found and put out the fire.

In early lookout history lookouts were placed ten to twenty miles apart so they could see the same fire and accurately triangulate its location. With the development of better radio communication, mapping systems and aerial detection, the need for as many lookouts is no longer as great. The 1950s was the peak decade for the number of working fire lookouts throughout the country, and the number of fire towers have been gradually decreasing ever since.

Although greatly diminished in number, the remaining five hundred fire lookouts continue to report the majority of wildfire throughout the nation's forests. In recent years, many inactive fire lookouts have been resurrected to help with fire spotting. In some locations, cameras as well as staffed lookout towers work together to report and triangulate wildfires.

1
HISTORY OF FIRE LOOKOUTS IN NEW MEXICO

At the turn of the twentieth century, the Manzano, Sandia, and Gallinas Mountains in central New Mexico were unsettled wilderness areas with no developed campgrounds and only primitive wagon roads and hunting trails traversing the isolated terrain. Resources on the forest were being indiscriminately used by early settlers and in an attempt to manage the land the Manzano Forest Reserve was established in 1906.

The passage of the Land Revision Act of 1891 authorized U.S. Presidents to set aside forest reserves. In 1907, the name forest reserve was changed to national forest. For the next twenty-four years the Manzano National Forest administered land not only in the Sandia and Manzano Mountains, but in the Zuni Range and Mt. Taylor Mountains near Grants, the Ladrone Range north of Socorro and portions of the Alamo Navajo Indian Reservation.

By 1909 ranger stations were constructed in Mountainair, Tajique and Hells Canyon. These first ranger stations were not much more than a primitive log cabin with a phone line strung to it for communication and corrals for the rangers' horses and pack string. It was not an easy job for these early rangers, as they were responsible for a vast acreage of land under management by the U.S. Government for the first time in its history.

The American public was not overly pleased initially with the establishment of national forests. Much of the forested land had been devastated by fire, timber and firewood were being removed at a steady rate and the land had been severely overgrazed by sheep and cattle. The first rangers were to gain control of the timber trade, decrease grazing permits and put out wildfire.

For a decade, Bosque Peak or El Bosque as it was called in its earlier history was the main observation point for the detection of forest fires in the Manzano Mountains. By 1912, officials in the Manzano National Forest had an operational phone line in service between Bosque Peak and the Tajique Ranger Station. In this pre-radio era, rangers strung primitive phone lines between the ranger stations and lookout points and communicated by phone and also by using flashing mirror signals in Morse code when not near a phone.

Archibald and Alice Rea homesteaded Bosque Ridge in the 1890s and were among the first to settle land within the Manzano Mountains. There was no road to the mountaintop when they decided to homestead the site, so Rea hired seventeen Pueblo Indians and built a wagon road ascending the ridge.

The Rea family established a profitable farm and ranch where they raised cattle and goats and enough vegetables to trade and see them through the year. Since the family had already built a good, wagon road to the top of Bosque Peak, the U.S. Forest Service decided to establish their first fire lookout station on the site and installed a phone line to the location.

According to an article in the *Albuquerque Herald* dated July 18, 1912, the Rea Ranch was helpful in reporting wildfire, "Supervisor Calkins says the lookout station on the Rea Ranch on top of Bosque

Ridge in the Manzanos proved valuable in detecting incipient fires and making possible their extinction before any damage was done."

Other lookout points used by the U.S. Forest Service during this era were Manzano Peak on the south end of the range where a tent was set up for the ranger on duty. Guadalupe Peak on the north end of the range was another lookout point where a pole tower was constructed and a tent supplied nearby for the ranger's cooking and sleeping needs.

The first official lookout station was erected on Capilla Peak in 1922 after the U.S. Forest Service decided to abandon the site on Bosque Peak. Capilla Peak being more centrally located had always been considered the more favorable lookout location in the Manzano Range. Material for a phone line was transported seven miles from the Tajique-Bosque line and a phone installed at the new lookout cabin on the peak.

The first lookout on Capilla Peak was a large, ponderosa pine tree with the top removed for easier access. Juan Chavez from Torreon was one of the first ranger/patrolman assigned to Capilla Peak. He provided his own horse and rode from Torreon most days and patrolled the peak, glassed for fire while sitting atop the large, pine tree and found and extinguished the fires he spotted. During this era in fire observation history, the fire lookout was required to find and put out the fires he spotted.

The 1920s lookout structure was removed in 1963 and replaced with the current lookout station. The lookout cab was transported to the top of the peak in the back of a truck where it was put atop a concrete base already in place. Mountainair District Ranger Bill Buck, Manuel Chavez, Joe Romero and T.J. Archuleta erected the new lookout on the peak.

The steep road to Capilla Peak Lookout was first open to the public in 1936. The Civilian Conservation Corps under the supervision of the U.S. Forest Service built the road to the top of the mountain range, as well as the original campground in 1937. An article in the *Albuquerque Journal* explains the road construction, "The road to Capilla partially constructed by CCC workers is sufficiently near completion to allow motorists to reach the summit."

One of the first lookouts to greet visitors at the top after the opening of the road was Colleen Johnson. She took care of spotting fires while Marvin Johnson, her husband was in charge of the crews building the original campground facilities. They lived at the lookout for the summer. There was a lot of activity on the peak in the 1930s as crews prepared the mountain summit for its first motorcar visitors.

Prior to this time, only two trails reached the crest of the Manzano Mountains. One trail followed the terrain for several miles from the Tajique Ranger Station to the crest, while the other trail was located between Torreon and the lookout site. The trail was never designated as an official trail but was used by crews after the installation of a telephone line to the original fire lookout. U.S. Forest Service crews referred to the trail as the "old telephone trail." The first fire lookouts communicated by telephone instead of radio and cell phone like today.

Another article in the *Albuquerque Journal* dated April 10, 1938 describes the direction of the road to the lookout tower, "The road to the peak passes through Manzano and New Canyon and then winds around the mountainside," the article pointed out. "Cars can be driven to the very summit of Capilla, which has parking space for five to six cars." The first year the road was open to the public cars were registered from Missouri, Colorado, Maryland, Texas, Arkansas and Arizona, as well as from over New Mexico.

The public was excited in the 1930s over the construction of Capilla Campground and the ability to drive to the summit of the Manzano Mountains. Completion of the road and campground were well publicized in area newspapers. The campground touted a continuous supply of spring water, a number of log table sets, fireplaces and three-sided log structures for the enjoyment of those members of the public brave enough to drive the somewhat treacherous road to the crest.

There were few locations for camping in the Manzano Mountains in the 1930s and the nearest overnight accommodations were in Mountainair, so the U.S. Forest Service with the help of Civilian Conservation Corps' crews stationed at Red Canyon constructed four well-equipped campgrounds including the one at Capilla. They were found in Tajique Canyon and at Red Canyon and Quarai now part of Salinas Pueblo Missions National Monument.

A true pioneer who worked for the U.S. Forest Service for forty years was Joe Romero from Mountainair. Firefighting techniques and responsibilities have changed since 1942 when Romero first started to fight wildfire. While modern firefighters use helicopters, chainsaws, cell phones and a GPS to determine the location of a fire, sixty years ago when Romero fought fires the tools were as rough as the terrain.

The 90-year-old, who is in amazingly good shape, had no trouble recalling facts from half a century earlier, "I loved the job and enjoyed working outdoors in the mountains all those years," he said. "There have been lots of improvements over the years, but I still think we caught our share of the fires."

One of Romero's first jobs with the U.S. Forest Service was repairing downed phone lines, the main form of communication between fire crews and lookouts in those days. "There were phone lines in the fire lookouts and ranger stations all the way to Chilili and Tijeras Canyon," Romero explained, "My brother and I worked together splicing and clamping lines. I usually walked while he drove."

The first roads in the Manzano Mountains were wagon roads and trails making it difficult for firefighters to reach the fires they fought. "We always expected a long hike," Romero pointed out. There was usually a patrolman or two on the crest who would initial attack the fire while we hiked to it. Back then, they thought nothing of one person working on a fire alone all day."

"The first couple years I worked for the Forest Service, the Civilian Conservation Corps had a camp in Red Canyon west of Mountainair," he said. "They helped build some of the early trails and campgrounds in the area and fought fires during the summer months. The camp was eventually removed."

"We never lost a fire in the Manzanos, because we got on them quickly and kept them small," Romero said. "It was dry in the 1950s and we had a lot of small fires. We stayed on them until they were completely dead and hiked out the next day. We did lose a few fires in the Gallinas though, as we sure did lose the Gallinas Fire in the 1970s. People could see that fire all the way from Alamogordo."

Original Lookout built at Capilla Lookout in 1922.
(Courtesy U.S. Forest Service)

Also making up land administered by the Mountainair District are the Gallinas Mountains west of Corona. The mountain range began its history with the U.S. Forest Service on November 5, 1906 when the Gallinas Forest Reserve was created. Two years later, the Gallinas National Forest was combined with the Lincoln National Forest and fifty years after that transferred to the Cibola National Forest where it has remained.

A telephone line was built to the top of Gallinas Peak in March of 1922 by Forest Examiner Burral and Ranger William H. Wood. The first years the lookout was staffed, the ranger/patrolman rode to the top of the ridge each day and glassed for fire but camped at Ranger Tank a few miles to the southwest probably because it would have been hard to haul water for his horse and pack animals. The first lookout structure on the peak was an early pole tower with an outside ladder for climbing to the top.

These early pole/platform style towers were not overly safe as described in a June 16, 1932 article in the *Alamogordo News*, "Ranger George Messer, of the Gallinas Station, reports to the Supervisor's Office that Paul Porter, fire guard in that district, has sustained painful injuries by falling from the ladder leading to the lookout tower last Saturday. The doctor says he will be able to work in about ten days."

The U.S. Forest Service decided to build a more permanent and safe tower as explained in the *Alamogordo News,* "The local supervisor's office has received notice by Aermotor Company of Chicago, of the shipment of two steel towers. One is 40 feet in height and will be placed at Gallinas Peak." The new lookout was erected on Gallinas Peak by Charles Pepper in June of 1933. The Gallinas Lookout site remains in use for the detection of forest fires. The Gallinas Tower is the oldest lookout structure still in service in the Cibola National Forest.

Gallinas Fire Lookout. (Courtesy Linda Powell)

Bill Buck served as the Mountainair District Ranger between 1961 and 1965 and left behind a wonderful memoir describing the techniques used by Joe Romero and Manuel Chavez, serving on the fire crew. Ranger Buck wrote, "To appreciate the dedication and devotion these men had for the ranger district and national forest, I'd like to repeat what George Schilling my good friend and predecessor told me once.

"Manuel was on the lookout and Joe was the smoke chaser at Tajique Cabin. Joe was searching for the smoke that Manuel had called in earlier in the day. It was getting dark and Joe was looking all over. He was climbing trees looking for the smoke drift, he smelled for smoke and listened for the sound of a fire crackling. Hours passed. No luck at all. Joe would drive all the ridge lines flashing his lights for Manuel to see. Finally, Manuel called Joe on the radio and says: Joe do you remember that little fire they had up here, that year when I was in the Army overseas and you didn't work for the Forest Service that year? Do you remember that fire? It was in one of those deep arroyos running off the southwest corner of Bosque? Joe says, yes I sure do. Manuel responds: This fire is right there, in that exact same spot. Joe drove to the spot and put the fire out. Joe and Manuel were probably the best two-man team that I'll ever know."

Cecilia Chavez staffing Capilla Lookout in 1963.
(Courtesy U.S. Forest Service)

Over a century after they were established, fire lookouts in the Cibola National Forest continue to play an important role in the detection of forest fires. Although advances in technology have replaced many fire towers throughout the country, the U.S. Forest Service continues to staff seven lookout towers in the Cibola National Forest each season between March and September.

The seven lookout towers are scattered throughout the Cibola National Forest. The Magdalena District staffs Withington Lookout in the San Mateo Mountains and Davenport Lookout near the small village of Datil in the Datil Mountains. The district also maintains Grassy Lookout to use during an extreme fire season.

The Mountainair District staffs Capilla Peak in the Manzano Mountains southeast of Albuquerque and Gallinas Lookout in the Gallinas Range near Corona.

Lookouts still in service on the Mt. Taylor District are: Oso Ridge in the Zuni Mountains, McGaffey Lookout near Gallup and La Mosca Lookout close to the summit of the Mt. Taylor Range.

Original Pole Tower at Cedro Lookout. (Courtesy U.S. Forest Service)

According to the *Las Cruces Sun News* on July 3, 1944, Mildred Swatzell was hired to staff Oso Ridge Lookout when her husband who had been hired for the position was rejected because of poor eyesight. Shortly after this photo was taken a beacon tower would be placed at the lookout site. Swatzell spent her days perched in a cabin part way up the airway beacon tower.

An article in the *Albuquerque Journal* dated May 7, 1944 had the following headline, "Woman Fire Lookout first to Spot Blaze."

The article went on to describe the fire, "Value of a woman fighting fires was demonstrated Saturday by Mrs. Mildred Swatzell who was the first to detect a fire in the lava beds southwest of Grants, Stanton Wallace of the Cibola National Forest reported. Mrs. Swatzell, who is one of two women lookouts serving in the area, spotted the fire from Oso Ridge and gave the alarm."

Mildred Swatzell staffing the original Oso Ridge Fire Lookout in 1944.
(Courtesy U.S. Forest Service)

Mrs. Richard Clawson also served as a fire lookout in the 1940s. Another article in the *Albuquerque Journal* dated March 25, 1943 gives a little background information, "Mrs. Richard Clawson, resident of many years in the vicinity of McGaffey, has been named forest fire lookout at the McGaffey Tower, U.S. Forest Service Cibola officials said Wednesday."

Although Mrs. Swatzell and Mrs. Clawson were touted in newspaper headlines as being the first women lookouts in the area, Lucy Whiteside served on Mt. Sedgwick over twenty years before either of them.

San Mateo Fire Lookout near Springtime Campground on the Magdalena District was an early pack in lookout where the lookout on duty spent months without leaving the lookout. The site has not been staffed since the 1970s. The stairs have been removed from the bottom of the lookout tower to keep visitors from climbing.

San Mateo Fire Lookout and Cabin. (Courtesy U.S. Forest Service)

Additional fire lookouts on the Magdalena District were primitive sites on South Baldy and Blue Mountain. Both appear to have been the platform, style lookout structure.

Mt. Sedgwick Fire Lookout in the Zuni Mountains was one of the first fire lookouts in the Cibola National Forest. The lookout is no longer used or standing, but fire crews continue to use the site as a lookout point when searching for a reported smoke. Lucy Whiteside was the first woman to staff a fire lookout in the Cibola National Forest when she took over the lookout duties on Mt. Sedgwick. Lucy staffed the lookout through the 1920 fire season.

Mount Sedgwick Fire Lookout is no longer standing.
(Courtesy U.S. Forest Service)

Five additional lookout sites were once in service in the area: Mt. Powell, Lookout Mountain, El Morro and Mt. Taylor Lookouts. The Acoma Reservation once staffed Brushy Lookout.

The Isleta Lookout Tower remains standing but has not been used for the detection of wildfire for the past fifteen years. Manzano Lookout to the north is utilized for training and fire-fighting scenarios but has not been a working lookout in decades.

Cedro Fire Lookout on the Sandia District also began its history as a pole tower. The lookout either rode horse back or hiked to the lookout each day from the Sandia Ranger Station. The pole tower was replaced with a new tower in the 1930s and used as a beacon tower by the Civil Aeronautics Authority (CAA).

When pilots first began to fly cross country, there were few navigational tools to help guide their way. During the daylight hours they used highway maps or looked out the window of their cockpits for landmarks. But there was nothing to guide them after dark. In 1919 crews lit large bonfires set along the route planes would fly. By 1923, lighted airport boundaries, spot-lit windsocks and rotating beacons were in place across the country to aid in flying during the evening hours.

Both Oso Ridge and Cedro Fire Lookouts served as beacon towers built by the CAA above their lookout structures. They became part of a transcontinental airway for pilots carrying mail 24 hours a day. These towers were placed every fifteen to twenty-five miles and adorned with a beacon powerful enough for pilots to see for at least forty miles on a clear night helping them to make it to their destinations.

By 1933, eighteen thousand miles of airways and fifteen hundred beacons were in place across the country. Each tower had site numbers painted on the top for identification during the daylight hours. At night, the beacons flashed in a sequence known by the pilots to identify their location. In addition to the rotating beacons, one fixed tower light pointed to the next field and another to the previous field forming an aerial roadway.

Beacon Tower atop Oso Ridge Lookout. (Courtesy U.S. Forest Service)

HISTORY OF SMOKEY BEAR AND LOOKOUTS IN NEW MEXICO'S LINCOLN NATIONAL FOREST

On a hot windy day in May of 1950, Block Fire Lookout Bob Latham reported the 17,000-acre Capitan Gap Fire. In no time, dry conditions combined with seventy mile per hour wind gusts blew the fire out of control and whirling dust clouds obscured the view. An hour after reporting the blaze, Latham told the dispatcher, "I can't see a thing, but I can smell it and it sure smells like a big one."

Block/Smokey Bear Fire Lookout. (Courtesy U.S. Forest Service)

The blaze was so fast moving that a group of firefighters was caught in its path and had to take shelter in a rock slide while the fire burned over them. Fortunately, they all survived with only minor burns along with singed hair and clothing. After the fire passed, they heard squeals and cries coming from a young bear cub clinging to a tree.

The wounded bear was taken into fire camp where his injuries were treated, and at first the firefighters referred to him as Hot Foot Teddy. The orphan cub not only won the hearts of his rescuers but of the American public as they came to know the tragic story of Smokey Bear.

The next day, Homer Pickens and Ray Bell of the New Mexico Department of Game and Fish took charge of the bear cub. Bell, a pilot flew Smokey to Santa Fe by placing him in a shoebox on the seat next to him. The cub was taken to Ed Smith's veterinarian hospital where his burns and wounds were extensively treated.

For two months while authorities decided what to do with the cub, Bell's wife and daughter nursed Smokey back to health. At first, the young bear had trouble eating but finally learned how to keep food down when given a mixture of honey, milk and baby food he sucked off the family's fingers. After a while, the cub played with the Bell's puppy and the two ate out of the same food dish.

The U.S. Forest Service decided to adopt the orphan bear and use in their ongoing fire prevention campaign. The agency had been using a fictional bear, but many felt a live bear especially one that had survived a forest fire would add to the campaign's effectiveness. The cub was flown to the National Zoo in Washington, DC where he would live until his death 26 years later.

The Piper Aircraft Company volunteered to transport Smokey to Washington, DC. A brand-new plane was sent to transport the bear cub and Frank Hines from Hobbs agreed to be the pilot. Homer Pickens was chosen to escort and take care of Smokey on his trip. Before the plane took off, a Santa Fe artist painted a picture of Smokey on the fuselage with his arm in a sling.

The first stop on their way to Washington was Amarillo, Texas. A crowd of spectators and newspaper reporters met the plane as everyone wanted a glimpse of the infamous bear. Even larger crowds were waiting in Tulsa, Kansas City, and Chicago as Smokey's story spread across the country. The American public loved the idea of Smokey Bear from the beginning, and because of him the U.S. Forest Service's prevention campaign took hold especially among children.

The U.S. Forest Service in conjunction with the military organized the first fire prevention campaign during World War II after a Japanese submarine shelled the California coast near Santa Barbara and continued to launch thousands of fire balloons over forests in the western United States. The uneasiness of the American public prompted the U.S. Forest Service to utilize their fire lookout stations to watch for incoming Japanese balloons and submarine activity and to maintain fire patrols throughout the year.

The first Smokey Bear poster was printed in 1944 showing a bear pouring a bucket of water over a campfire with the caption, "Care will prevent 9 out of 10 fires." By 1947, Smokey Bear posters touted the familiar phrase still used by the U.S. Forest Service, "Only you can prevent forest fires." The small, bear cub found in New Mexico's Capitan Mountains greatly added to the success of the agency's fire prevention campaign.

When Smokey Bear passed away in 1976 his remains were returned to the Capitan Mountains of his birth. His body was flown from Washington, DC to Albuquerque in a pine box painted green where his remains were transported by caravan to his final resting place in Capitan.

Smokey is buried in the Smokey Bear Historical Park where visitors often stop and visit his grave and read about his life. The staff at the park recently completed an exhibit on Bob Latham and the Block Fire Lookout finally giving Latham credit for his contributions as a fire lookout. The visitor center at the park is full of Smokey Bear posters, memorabilia, photos, and informative information about the young bear cub that made history.

Soon after the fire, a movement began to change the names of businesses and forest landmarks to Smokey Bear. In 1959, the names of the Block Lookout, Capitan Ranger Station and Capitan Gap were changed to Smokey Bear. Local businesses also changed their names to the Smokey Bear Café, Smokey Bear Motel and more. The spirit of Smokey Bear continues to live on throughout the Capitan Mountains.

NOTE: For a more detailed account of the story of Smokey Bear, see *Smokey Bear and the Great Wilderness* by Elliott S. Barker, Sunstone Press, 1982.

Bob Latham worked at the Block Fire Tower for twenty-five years between 1932 and 1957. His career with the U.S. Forest Service included five years as the Civilian Conservation Corps foreman. According to the *Alamogordo Daily News* in August of 1957, "Long before the present tower was built, Bob lived at the old station and walked on foot up to the knoll where the lookout cab now stands."

Bob Latham and wife Estelle. (Courtesy Paul Wild)

When Bob was asked why he was retiring he stated, "Through the years the lookout work has changed from spotting fires and traveling horseback to put them out to the present-day direction of fire crew activities by means of radio. It's time for a change." The lookout structure was demolished in the 1960s when a prehistoric Native American pueblo was discovered on the site leaving no lookout stations on the north side of the Capitan Mountains.

One of the most picturesque lookouts in the Lincoln National Forest is Monjeau Fire Lookout. It was designed by architect Ellis Groben who believed in using natural materials in a harmonious style. He wanted the lookout to have a distinct character that blended with the location. The lookout site, being near Ruidoso and Ski Apache, is quite popular with the public and receives thousands of visitors each month. Monjeau Lookout was placed on the National Register of Historic Places in 1988.

Monjeau Fire Lookout. (Courtesy U.S. Forest Service)

Possibly the oldest lookout site on the Lincoln National Forest is the Russia Lookout Tree. The El Paso & Southwestern Railroad Company built track into the Sacramento Mountains in the 1880s and the small settlement of Russia became a location for bringing out the logs and transporting them to where crews were building track.

The settlement was located five miles east of Cloudcroft and named Russia because of the severe winters. The pioneer settlement had a post office between 1904 and 1906. A fire patrolman often staffed the lookout tree overlooking the railroad's timber supply during the years the settlement existed and was responsible for reporting and extinguishing the fires he saw.

The rescue of Smokey Bear started a fire prevention movement continued to the present day. Replicas of Smokey Bear greet visitors at ranger stations and national forests throughout the country and most school children know his name and story. The young bear cub born in New Mexico's Capitan Mountains touched the hearts of those who knew him. He was the perfect symbol to use for fire prevention and was the most popular exhibit at the National Zoo during his stay there.

The Lincoln National Forest no longer staffs their lookout sites and has started to use cameras instead of fire lookouts for the detection of wildfire.

Smokey Bear Historical Park. (Courtesy Dixie Boyle)

THE GILA NATIONAL FOREST AND NEW MEXICO'S MOST REMOTE FIRE LOOKOUTS

Fire Lookouts in the Gila National Forest are some of the most remote lookouts in the Southwest. The Gila is wide, open country full of elk and other wildlife with few roads and rugged landscapes. It is the largest forest in New Mexico and the sixth largest in the continental United States. The Gila Wilderness turned one hundred years old in 2024 and holds the distinction of being the first designated wilderness in the country.

Naturalist Aldo Leopold was passionate about preserving the country's remaining wilderness areas and was instrumental in the establishment of the Gila Wilderness in 1924. The Aldo Leopold Wilderness was established in 1980 and is often described as New Mexico's most remote corner.

The Gila continues to staff ten fire lookouts each fire season, the most of any forest in the state. Most of the sites are staffed by long-term employees who have worked the lookouts for twenty years or more. Hillsboro Peak, Black Mountain and Mogollon Baldy Lookouts are three of the most isolated lookouts in the state and require a three-to-twelve-mile hike to reach the lookout sites.

Mogollon Baldy, located in the Gila Wilderness, is not only the highest lookout in the Gila at 10,770 feet but is also New Mexico's most remote lookout station. The lookout is located seventy-five miles northwest of Silver City, and then another twelve-mile hike to reach the lookout station. Sara Irving has staffed Mogollon Baldy for over forty years making her one of the longest working fire lookouts in the nation.

Original Mogollon Baldy Fire Lookout in the Gila Wilderness.
(Courtesy U.S. Forest Service)

Mogollon Baldy has been used for the spotting of forest fires since 1913. At that time smoke chasers rode to the site each day on horse-back and when spotting a fire used a protractor on a tree stump to triangulate its location. In 1924 a wooden tower was erected and used until the present tower was built in 1948.

Phil Connors, author of the award-winning lookout book *Fire Season: Field Notes from a Wilderness Lookout,* has staffed Hillsboro Peak for over twenty years and considers the mountain top his summer home. He left a prestigious job with the *Wall Street Journal* in 2002 when offered the job at Hillsboro Peak and has staffed the lookout ever since.

The original lookout structure on Hillsboro Peak was a wooden lookout tower erected circa 1915. One of the first lookouts to staff the lookout was Kingston resident Cecilia Anderson. When not staffing the lookout, she lived in a dugout on the site before a cabin was built.

Cecilia Anderson at Hillsboro Peak in 1922.
(Courtesy U.S. Forest Service)

The final pack-in lookout is Black Mountain located along the northern edge of the Gila Wilderness. Those staffing the lookout leave their vehicle at the Beaverhead Work Center and hike the three miles to the lookout site. The present lookout structure was erected in 1934.

Raymond Schmidt was an early fire lookout and smoke chaser on Lookout Mountain on the Black Range District when the forest was still named the Datil National Forest. Schmidt self-published a delightful book named *New Mexico Recollections* about his experiences fighting and reporting forest fires.

Schmidt was required to report as well as extinguish the fires he reported. He remained in the wilderness most of his tour and packed in water and supplies by pack mule. It was not uncommon for these first fire lookouts to not only build the lookouts they would staff but surrounding trails and roads as well.

Schmidt spent eight years staffing Lookout Mountain. He writes about the lookout, "In the year 1914, when I was seventeen years old, I hiked to the top of Lookout Mountain and found there Hugh McTavish, B.F. Daniel, and Forest Ranger L.J. Mundel. They were erecting the first tower that I was to occupy for eight fire seasons."

Prior to this time, B.F. Daniel the first person to staff the lookout site used a ponderosa pine tree for the detection of forest fires. Hugh Mactavish was a prospector in the area who just happened by that day and was helping with the construction of the lookout tower. The job was offered to Schmidt when Daniel decided not to return in 1917.

Original Crow's Nest Lookout at Lookout Mountain.
(Courtesy U.S. Forest Service)

Not only did these early fire lookouts have to take care of themselves in the wilderness for months at a time, but they were also charged with the care of their horses and pack animals. The rangers and smoke chasers were on constant alert for mountain lions, grizzlies, and other wildlife that might attack their animals.

Schmidt was relaxing one evening after putting out a small fire when he discovered cougar tracks near the trail. After closely examining the tracks, it appeared the animal had waited for him in the brush. He described hearing the screams of cougars during his stay on the lookout upsetting his horses. Fire Lookouts of this era had to be constantly on alert for more than wildfire.

Eagle Peak Fire Lookout, located on the Reserve District, has one of the best views in the Gila National Forest. As its name suggests the lookout has a bird's eye view of the surrounding landscape. One of the longest working lookout personnel on Eagle Peak was H.B. Birmingham who had a ranch near the lookout site. H.B.'s dad Henry Birmingham worked the lookout before him in the 1920s.

The first five years H.B. lived at the lookout, his wife Peggy served as the fire lookout and H.B. as the smoke chaser, which was a common practice during these years. H.B. knew the country well and was often described as a walking history book. His wife Peggy was affectionately called Aunt Peggy by those who knew her.

The Quemado Ranger District near the Arizona border staffs Fox Mountain and Mangas Fire Lookouts. Both have been lookout sites since the 1920s. The present lookout on Fox Mountain was built in 1959. Mangas Lookout was erected in 1934 and replaced an earlier platform/pole tower used at the site.

While staffing the pole tower at Mangas Lookout in 1924, lookout Willis Bitmore and a companion were struck by lightning. The bolt instantly killed Bitmore but knocked his companion unconscious. When he recovered, he discovered Bitmore was dead and the phone lines had been damaged by the lightning as well. He caught his horse and rode the five miles to the ranger station in order to report the tragedy.

Signal Peak Fire Lookout is located in the Pinos Altos Mountains north of Silver City and is a popular location for hikers and mountain bikers. The lookout was first staffed in 1933. The original cab of the lookout was replaced in 1966. It provides an endless view of the surrounding landmarks.

Bearwallow Fire Lookout in 1982. (Courtesy Dixie Boyle)

Bearwallow and Saddle Mountain Lookouts are part of the Glenwood Ranger District. The present lookout on Saddle Mountain was built in 1966 replacing an earlier lookout. Bearwallow was erected in 1923.

An article in the *Albuquerque Journal* dated June 6, 1913 tells of the importance of staffing the Bearwallow Lookout site. Supervisor Johnson had recently returned to Silver City by team and wagon after helping to fight the fire reported by the Bearwallow Lookout.

The article states, "The discovery of the fire is a credit to the efficiency of the fire lookout service, for it was located in a place where it would ordinarily have burned a couple weeks before being discovered and would have caused a lot more problems."

Ten more lookout sites were once active in the Gila National Forest: Boiler Peak cabin, Diamond Peak, El Caso, Granite Peak, Negrito Lookout, Reeds Peak, Wagon Tongue, Grouse Mountain, Highland Park, and John Kerr. They were all Crow's Nests or Aermotors with a ground cabin for the lookout on duty and corrals for the pack string. Most of the former lookout sites in the Gila have been demolished. Many of these sites were similar to Highland Park Fire Lookout established as a Crow's Nest in 1917.

Highland Park Lookout site in 1921 (Courtesy U.S. Forest Service)

THE CARSON AND SANTA FE NATIONAL FORESTS

For over a decade, the Carson National Forest in northern New Mexico has relied upon aerial and ground patrols; as well as, cell phone users for the reporting of wildfire. The Forest no longer staffs the two lookout towers that remain standing: Kiowa and Picuris Lookouts. Both lookouts were regularly staffed into the 1990s.

Shortly after the Canjilion District was organized in 1909, the first fire lookout was put into operation. The lookout site was primitive by modern standards with a wooden platform open to the elements and a small cabin nearby. The lookout was removed in the 1920s but the cabin remains at the location and was listed on the National Register of Historic Places in 1988 and named the Victor Ortega Cabin.

The lookout was in service for fifteen years between 1909 and 1924 when Victor Ortega the lookout on duty was struck and killed by lightning in front of his family. After the tragic incident, the U.S. Forest Service decided to discontinue using the location and abandoned the lookout site.

During the time Ortega worked the lookout his duties were a little different from the present-day duties of fire lookouts. He was required to patrol the rim of the mountain for three miles every two hours while watching for smoke and when one was spotted, he extinguished it. The rest of the time he remained near a telephone in order to give cross reading on fires from other lookouts.

An article in the *Albuquerque Journal* dated July 22, 1911 tells of building a fire lookout on San Antone Mountain but the lookout is not listed as a lookout a few years later. The article stated, "A Forest Service line is under construction to connect with the forest telephone that runs to Canjilion and in a few days will begin the construction of a line to San Antone Mountain where a lookout station for forest fires will be established."

The Canjilion Fire Lookout cabin was constructed in 1909.
(Courtesy U.S. Forest Service)

By the 1960s the Carson National Forest staffed three lookout stations: Kiowa, Picuris, and Carracas. It appears that Canjilion and San Antone Mountain may have been replaced by these later lookouts and built in better locations for the observation of wildfire.

Picuris Fire Lookout is located between Taos and Penasco and has an amazing view of the Colorado border country as well as Los Alamos and the land beyond. Eli Romero worked the lookout the longest of any lookout personnel, as he accepted the lookout position in 1958. The lookout being on a main road had a lot of visitors as well as fires.

Picuris Fire Lookout in the 1940s. (Courtesy U.S. Forest Service)

Kiowa Fire Lookout, located between Vallecitos and Tres Piedras is on the El Rito District. O.A. Washburn worked the lookout in 1968 and left behind a description of his job, "It was my good fortune as a young man to have a fire lookout job with the U.S. Forest Kiowa Lookout 15 miles west of Tres Piedras."

Most of the early lookouts could only be reached by foot or horse trail, and these first lookouts received few visitors. Washburn spent most of the summer alone communing with the wildlife and made pets out of a few of the animals that visited his lookout tower.

He tells of going for weeks with no visitors. He became so lonely that he started to cultivate animal companionships. He wrote, "I had a number of such wild friends that visited regularly: rabbit, foxes, chipmunks, bears, deer, porcupines, skunks, and birds of all kinds."

Eleanor Daggett tells about staffing Kiowa Lookout in the *Santa Fe New Mexican* dated June 18, 1972. She and her husband staffed the lookout for several summers in the 1970s. He worked as the smoke chaser and she served as the fire lookout. She wrote, "Great granite boulders cover the top of the peak. The spine-chilling metal ladder up the side has been replaced by a central winding staircase," she explained. "From the tower you meet the rising sun and the Sangre de Cristos at eye level. You know Taos lies over there at the foot of the Sangres."

Daggett loved wildflowers and spent much of her time identifying those on the peak. While on the lookout she devoted her time to learning the names of the flowers in earnest and collecting specimens.

Kiowa Fire Lookout in 1938. (Courtesy U.S. Forest Service)

Jack and Jean Loeffler from California was the first couple to staff Carracas Peak Lookout in 1965. They spent several summers at the site while researching a book on Native American tribes of North America. During this era the U.S. Forest Service wanted to establish living quarters at their lookout sites. An article in the *Albuquerque Journal* dated August 10, 1965 explains, "The Loefflers represented what was the first step by the Forest Service in establishing what is expected to be permanent living quarters for someone who will maintain a new fire lookout in the Carson National Forest." Jack was paid for five days a week and Jean for two.

The life on the lookout was not always easy. The couple packed water to the lookout from a spring two miles away. They used 20 gallons every three days, so it became an important job for one of them more than once a week.

When the couple was not looking for fires, they took hikes or occupied themselves with their project in researching Native Americans. With the money they earned during their first summer on the lookout, they traveled to Oaxaca, Mexico and spent the winter studying the Native Americans there.

The Loefflers had started their research project the summer before and lived with a Navajo family near Navajo Mountain in Utah. They got along so well with the family that they adopted them and even gave them their own Hogan. Jack Loeffler would go on to write books, work as a film and radio producer and become a respected author and historian.

Loeffler was also a good friend of the author Edward Abbey. He helped to bury his friend at an unknown location in the mountains near Tucson as Abbey had requested. He promised Abbey he would never tell anyone where he was buried. He wrote about his friendship with Abbey in his book *Adventures with Ed.*

Barillas Fire Lookout after the Fire. (Courtesy U.S. Forest Service)

The Santa Fe National Forest is down to three active fire lookouts after the Hermits Peak/Calf Canyon Fire in 2022 damaged the cab of the Barillas Fire Lookout. The Pecos District does plan on replacing the fire lookout in the future but at the time of the publication of this book, the lookout structure is fenced off from the public and not in use.

As most lookout sites Barillas Peak had more than one fire lookout. The present-day lookout was built upon the peak in 1959 and served until 2022. The first lookout to staff the new tower was Tony Vigil. Vigil enjoyed the new lookout tower with windows all around. The lookout was furnished with a wood stove and two twin beds and a Coleman lantern to provide light.

Although Barillas had been considered as the primary fire lookout, in the 1970s Glorieta Baldy took over that position and Barillas was staffed on an intermittent basis. Many years an observer was sent to the site only if there had been fires or lightning, but the lookout site retained its primary basis in later years when the U.S. Forest Service decided to close the Glorieta Baldy Lookout site.

Cerro Pelado Fire Lookout. (Courtesy U.S. Forest Service)

Cerro Pelado has served as a fire lookout on the Jemez District since 1913. Simon Sandavol staffed the lookout site for at least thirty years starting in the 1930s through the 1950s. His wife and son spent most of the season atop the mountain with him. Simon kept three of his own horses in a pasture near the lookout. He would use the horses to respond to fires in the vicinity of the lookout tower.

In 1948 two Catholic priests named Father James Armitage and John Buckley served as lookouts on Cerro Pelado. The priests were good lookouts and enjoyed taking a break from their work and meditating when not on duty. The priests took turns staffing the fire lookout while the other worked on the maintenance of the lookout site. The two cleared the telephone trails, repaired the lookout shutters and installed new stone steps up to the lookout and made sure the flagpole was painted. The present lookout was erected on the site in the early 1960s.

Deadman Fire Lookout. (Courtesy U.S. Forest Service)

The Deadman Fire Lookout remains an active lookout in the Santa Fe National Forest and is staffed each fire season. Most historians believe the lookout received its name from a dead man found on the site. An article in the *Jemez Forest Ranger* tells the story, "Assistant Ranger Sypher reports that on May 11, while riding his lookout points, he found the headless corpse of a man which from all appearances had lain there for six months. The skull bones were scattered and broken and when placed together showed a bullet in the back." It seems this site was originally called Gallina Mountain Lookout but by 1924 the lookout was called Deadman. Deadman has always been an active fire lookout. The lookout remains in communication not only with the Santa Fe National Forest but also the Carson and the Jicarilla Apache Indian Reservation.

Ben Casaus temporarily worked at the site late in the fire season of 1960. He actually drove his Volkswagon Beetle to the top of the mountain with his wife and two children. While they staffed the lookout a massive snow storm passed over the area and dropped 14 inches. The fire patrolman's truck got stuck, but the lookout was able to get out in Volkswagen and even pull the truck out.

Encino Fire Lookout. (Courtesy U.S. Forest Service)

Encino Fire Lookout is part of the Coyote Ranger District and is consistently staffed each fire season. The steel tower at the site is labeled USFS Grand Canyon, Arizona and was originally erected at Skinner Ridge on the Kaibab National Forest and was abandoned but still standing in 1941. The Santa Fe was able to obtain the lookout structure in the late 1940s. In early 1950 Wayne Wasson and a Mr. Young assembled it on the site. Two cabins from Cerro Valdez were moved to Encino in 1949 and the site has severed as a primary fire lookout ever since.

The first person to staff Encino was Felix Garcia. Uvaldo Velasquez served as the fire patrolman at the site while Garcia staffed the fire tower. By 1957 Velasquez had taken over the lookout duties at the location.

When Jose Endalesmo Trujillo began working as the lookout at Encino in the early sixties, he still had to ride a horse up the trail from the Ranger Station then located in the small town of Coyote. There had been a road constructed to the lookout but it was very rough and hard to travel and issues with the right of way delayed the opening of the road until 1966.

The main source used for information on the lookouts in the Santa Fe National Forest was taken from the document *Fire Lookout History of the Santa Fe National Forest* by Barb Zinn. Barb lost her lookout Barillas in the Hermit's Peak/Calf Canyon Fire and at the time of the publication of this book staffs a lookout in Arizona. She watched the fire for three weeks before evacuating then saw it burn over and destroy the lookout.

NEW MEXICO'S STATE FORESTRY LOOKOUTS

There were once five State Forestry Fire Lookouts staffed throughout the state. They were: Luera Peak in Catron County, Armstrong a military portable, Oscura Peak an Aermotor now on the White Sands Bombing Range, White Peak in Colfax County, and the Turkey Lookout Tower overlooking the town of Cimarron in the northern section of the state.

Luera Peak, a crow's nest style lookout was in service for twenty years atop Luera Mountain in Catron County in southwestern New Mexico. The lookout site is forty air miles from Magdalena. Not only was the lookout unusual but considered precarious and unsafe. No one had ever been hurt while staffing the lookout but several had slipped on their way down.

The lookout would definitely be considered unsafe by today's standards. The top was cleared from a 35-foot pine tree where a wooden platform was placed and a metal, office chair attached. There were no guard rails around the structure and the whole contraption wobbled when staffed.

The chair faced south and the lookout was able to easily scan to the south, east and west without too much difficulty, but had to turn completely around to look north causing the structure to lean precariously to one side.

When a fire was spotted, the lookout on duty had to scramble down 36 steps and rush to a tree stump where a direction finder was located. The direction finder was usually inaccurate and difficult to pinpoint a fire if it was more than five miles away. Then the lookout shimmied back up the tree in order to report the fire. The 36-foot tower was a little too low to see wildfire at any distance from the lookout, so the lookout climbed back down the structure to patrol the mountain looking for fire.

State Forester Manuel Ortiz stated in a newspaper article, "We've been afraid for years that we'll have a calamity up there." He was afraid someone would tumble right off the lookout tower. Several newspapers in 1971 criticized the primitive lookout structure and stated it was not safe.

Ortiz felt a new tower was desperately needed at the site and convinced then Governor Bruce King to petition the New Mexico Legislature three times for money to build a 60-foot Aermotor type lookout at the site in 1972, 1973 and 1974. A bill giving $37,000 for the lookout died in the Senate Finance Committee without receiving a hearing.

In 1975, the New Mexico State Forestry was forced to use the metal office chair for spotting forest fires. Ortiz pointed out in an interview, "We have no choice. We will have to continue using it, but we'll use it as little as possible." This would be the last year the Forestry Department used the lookout structure. Hopes of replacing the fire spotting perch were dashed by the state legislature and the lookout site was no longer staffed.

White Peak Fire Lookout – Colfax County – New Mexico
(Courtesy National Historic Lookout Register)

NEW MEXICO RESERVATION FIRE LOOKOUTS

Mt. Powell was the first lookout erected on the Navajo Reservation and the first to go out of service. The lookout has not been staffed since the 1970s and is no longer standing. Three other lookouts remain semi-active on the Navajo Reservation. Mt. Washington, an Aermotor style lookout, stands 81 feet high. The lookout site is the highest lookout in elevation on the reservation, located in the Chuska Mountains and built in 1936.

Mt. Powell Fire Lookout on the Navajo Reservation.
(Courtesy Dave Lorenz)

Tohnitsha Lookout was also built in 1936 and is an 82-foot Aermotor. The final lookout on the Navajo Reservation is Tohatchi Lookout. The lookout was built in 1928 making it the oldest lookout on the Navajo Reservation. The lookout stands 62 feet high.

Four fire lookouts remain active on the Jicarilla Apache Reservation in the northern section of the state. The lookouts still staffed are: Atole, Cedar Springs, Osborn, and Wells. Atole Lookout was built by the USFS to serve on Devil Mountain Lookout in Colorado's San Juan Mountains. When it was declared surplus, the BIA claimed it and in 1996 the lookout was moved by helicopter in three different trips by the Nevada National Guard. It was moved to the lookout location on Tecote Mesa.

Cedar Springs Lookout was erected in 1955 with a two-room ground cabin living quarters nearby. Osborne Lookout was built in 1960 and is located on Archuleta Mesa. Wells Lookout has been used as an observation point since 1930. The lookout site was erected in 1932.

Until the early 2000s the Mescalero Apache Reservation near Ruidoso in southern New Mexico staffed five fire towers each fire season. These former lookout sites were: Cienegita, Five Mile, Harley Mountain, Pajarita Mountain and Silver lookout towers. The lookouts, severely vandalized more than once throughout their history, are no longer staffed but remain standing. Two other lookouts in the area were also mentioned in newspaper articles called Nogal and Carrizo Lookouts. There is not much information on these two lookouts and they were probably not much more than a crow's nest type lookout and are no longer standing.

The Mescalero Indian Reservation was established by then President Ulysses Grant in 1873. Several mountain tops near the reservation are considered the sacred mountains of the tribe. These mountains are: Sierra Blanca, Guadalupe Mountain, Three Sisters Mountain, and Oscura Peak in the Oscura Range south of Highway 380 running between San Antonio near Interstate 25 and Carrizozo.

2
HISTORY OF FIRE LOOKOUTS IN THE BLACK HILLS NATIONAL FOREST, WYOMING AND SOUTH DAKOTA

The Black Hills fire lookouts, located in Wyoming and South Dakota are magical sites overlooking a landscape full of frontier history. A few of the historic landmarks making up the region are Deadwood where Wild Bill Hickok's short life ended, Bear Butte the sacred mountain of the Plains tribes, Black Elk Peak (formerly Harney Peak), the highest point east of the Rocky Mountains and Inyan Kara where General George Armstrong Custer and a few of his troops hiked to the top and carved the name Custer in a rock at the crest.

The top of Inyan Kara was never used as an official lookout site except by the Sioux tribe when they inhabited the landscape. Inyan Kara Mountain stands between Sundance and Newcastle, Wyoming. General George Armstrong Custer climbed Inyan Kara in 1874. Large grass fires set by the Sioux under Red Cloud obscured their view. The Sioux were hoping to scare off the expedition.

An article in the *Rapid City Journal* dated December 7, 1938 tells of the establishment of the Black Hills National Forest, "The Black Hills was made a national preserve by proclamation of President Grover Cleveland in 1877. Seth Bullock served as the first supervisor until 1902, when he was succeeded by John Fremont Smith. In 1907 the name was changed from preserve to Black Hills National Forest. In 1911 the forest was divided into the Black Hills and Harney National Forests, with headquarters for the Black Hills at Deadwood and at Custer for the Harney."

During the heyday years of standing fire lookouts in the 1950s, the Black Hills National Forest had twenty-four fire lookouts scattered throughout the Black Hills area. Six fire lookouts remain in service: Warren Peak, Cement Ridge, Custer Peak, Elk Mountain and Bear Mountain are staffed by the U.S. Forest Service and Mt. Coolidge is administered by Custer State Park.

Fires were so out of control throughout the Black Hills at the turn of the 20th Century that many people began pushing for fire lookout stations to help pinpoint the fires when they were smaller and easy to control. According to the *Custer County Chronicle* in April 1909, "The Forest Service men in the Black Hills are agitating for the establishment of stations for fire patrol on Harney Peak and Terry Peak. It is a good scheme and we hope the Government will take cognizance of the importance of such stations and the advantage they may accrue there from a lookout on each peak provided with good field glasses can view the entire Hills territory and a phone line from each peak to the nearest established phone line in case of fire they can save valuable time in mobilizing to save property. The *Chronicle* deems this an imperative need and is willing to favor the project and urge its fulfillment. We hope the boys will keep urging the matter until they gain the object desired."

As early as the 1890s, the Black Hills were plagued with devastating fires. The Iron Creek Fire burned close to 20,000 acres in 1898. Much of the Limestone Range south of Custer was destroyed, and the McVey Fire could not be controlled for over four days in the 1930s.

The U.S. Forest Service began discussing the importance of constructing fire lookouts in the Black Hills in 1909, but the first lookouts would not go up for another two years.

Harney Peak is credited with being the first to go into service, although the lookout site was not much more than a canvas tent with a wooden crate and an alidade to pinpoint forest fires.

Custer Peak, Cement Ridge, and Bear Mountain also went into service later in the fire season with primitive wooden lookout towers. Roads were built to the sites and all three became primary lookouts and currently remain in that status. Shortly after Harney Peak went into service, a wooden platform or crow's nest was completed on Bear Mountain.

There have been many dedicated lookouts on Bear Mountain over the years, but one of the most dedicated was a lookout named Gail Duncan Herbert. She worked as a fire lookout in the Black Hills for thirty-five years between 1946 and 1981.

Gail staffed several different lookouts in the Black Hills. She spent her first few years as a lookout on Parker Peak, a lookout site that no longer exists between Edgemont and Hot Springs, South Dakota.

In Gail's own words taken from an article in the *Rapid City Journal* dated August 11, 1981, "In those days you were on contract. You had to get your own food, water and wood rustled up. No man came up and cut it for you. We cooked everything on the woodstove."

Another quote by Gail summarizes the lookout experience for those who spend decades on a fire lookout, "You have to sacrifice everything to be a good lookout and have to dearly love the old country. You're always looking. I'd sure hate to have someone pick up a smoke on me. Sure, I am going to miss the Black Hills. As hard as anything will be getting back into the swing of the public, and I don't think you can run away from the busy world. You know Edna Allen, an old fire watch friend, used to say you had to be nuts to do this. When you get down in the fall you are happy, but after a week you're crazy."

The *News-Letter Journal* newspaper in Newcastle printed information about the Bear Mountain Lookout in 1919, "The dry weather has increased the fire hazard and Mr. Michaud has been assigned to lookout duty on Bear Mountain. Lookouts will now be maintained on both Harney Peak and Bear Mountain until the end of the season."

The *Rapid City Journal* dated July 22, 1939 explains the dismantling of the wooden lookout on Bear Mountain, "The old wooden tower at Bear Mountain, north of Custer, was dismantled and a 30-foot steel tower was raised in its place. George Stums is the lookout. Bear Mountain affords a view into the Limestone country, east to Harney Peak and south to Minnekahta."

The Bear Mountain Lookout site has been used for the detection of forest fires since circa 1910 when a platform/pole style tower was used by the first fire patrolmen scanning the forest. A cab was later added to the pole tower and renovated. It was used until 1939 when the present steel tower was erected on the site.

Bear Mountain Fire Lookout remains an active lookout each fire season. (Courtesy U.S. Forest Service)

First Platform Tower on Bear Mountain circa 1910.
(Courtesy U.S. Forest Service)

Bear Mountain Lookout circa 1917.
(Courtesy U.S. Forest Service)

Bear Mountain Lookout in 1924. (Courtesy U.S. Forest Service)

An article in the *Rapid City Journal* dated July 23, 1988 by Dick Willis tells of the lookout experience of Ed Cline who served on Bear Mountain. "The top of Bear Mountain is where lookout Ed Cline finds peace. Ed sits up there all day looking for forest fires. He doesn't have to do it. He doesn't even get paid for it. He does it just because he wants to."

Ed likes the people in western South Dakota. They're friendly. But to be honest about it, the fact we're all so friendly here isn't the main thing he likes about us. It's the fact there are so few of us that he likes best.

Ed explained how you always have to keep your eyes open. "I've got one of those swivel chairs. I turned from truck driver to swivel chair jockey. If you see something that is a little out of the way, then you take the binoculars and take a closer look."

Ed was a truck driver for thirty-five years. He and his wife have a 27-foot-long camping trailer. They stay the whole summer in the Black Hills, with Ed on the lookout. It's a long way from southern California.

"When we came up here in 1986 it was the first time we had come back in thirty years. We used to live in Nebraska, and we came up on our honeymoon. It hasn't changed much."

The first lookout stations on Custer Peak and Cement Ridge were completed near the same time as Harney Peak, and both of the sites have had three different lookout towers throughout their history. The first person to staff the Custer Peak Lookout was Black Hills native Frank Tower. Initially, the tower had telephone connections with the Deadwood office and other lookouts.

The Deadwood Pioneer-Times in March of 1911 tells of the construction of the first Custer Peak Lookout structure. "The wire and other materials for this station lie in Rochford and the work of installing the line will soon be undertaken. It will connect with the Nebraska Telephone Company's lines near the Bull Dog Ranch at Dumont."

The first primitive structure appeared on Custer Peak in 1911. The lookout site was named after General George Armstrong Custer. During the Black Hills Expedition of 1874 Custer and a few members of his expedition climbed to the top of Harney Peak (now Black Elk Peak). While on top they noticed two peaks in the distance and named one Custer Peak and the other Terry Peak. Their climbing adventure took most of the day and signal fires were lit from those camping at the base of the mountain to help them find their way back to camp in the dark. Custer and Harney were two of the first lookout sites in the Black

Hills. From reading newspapers of the era, it is obvious the people wanted fire lookouts to help protect the forest as well as their homes and communities.

Frank Tower was selected as the first person to staff the Custer Peak Lookout site. He had spent most of his life at the nearby Mountain Meadow Ranch and knew every gulch and mountain in the Black Hills. He reported the fires he discovered by telephone to the Deadwood Office, and the crews had little trouble finding the blazes in record time.

His family often joined him at the lookout and came close to being struck by lightning one afternoon when a major thunder storm formed over the top of the lookout tower. Frank was not at the tower, but his wife, child and sister-in-law were. They quickly headed for the root cellar and had barely entered when a bolt of lightning hit the lookout tower. The bolt was so powerful that it broke the windows, destroyed the telephone line, and scorched the lookout.

First Custer Peak Lookout built in 1911. (Courtesy U.S. Forest Service)

Tower had a harrowing experience in October of 1931 according to the *Argus-Leader* newspaper. Unfortunately, the article does not mention which fire blew up but tells of Tower's escape from the blaze. The fire broke out on a Thursday and Tower staffed the lookout until Saturday afternoon when the fire burned the phone lines.

The article tells of his experience, "Tower had orders from headquarters to stay at his station until the telephone line burned and then to make his way down the west slope of the mountain peak and meet up with M.R. Hickle who was in charge of fire-fighting operations on that side of the mountain."

Tower had remained at his lookout station throughout the fire. He reported to the forest office in Deadwood and to field telephones on the line about the progress of the fire; as well as, the locations of new blazes which were springing up everywhere he looked. Early in the afternoon, the telephone line began to buzz signaling the line had gone dead and he could do nothing more at his lookout station.

He had almost waited too late to leave the lookout as the fire cut off his path down the western slope of the mountain and he had to change course several times in order to avoid the blaze. The flames were racing up the hillside and making Tower uncomfortably hot. The fire began to jump over Tower and cut off his path in both directions.

In a final effort to avoid the fire, he was forced to cache his equipment in a culvert and run for his life. He made it to the highway unscathed and flagged down a truck going into Deadwood hauling supplies for the fire. The next morning, he worked on the fire line until he could return to his lookout.

According to the *Argus Leader* dated May 24, 1938 Tower was starting his 21st year staffing Custer Peak, "When Frank Tower rides his horse up the hill to the little glass enclosed house on Custer Peak it will be the 21st summer he has spent as fire lookout on the peak.

Tower goes up to the lookout station about May 1 usually and remains there until September 1 or longer if the fire hazard is apparent. Ordinarily the summer is pretty quiet he said.

The lookout station, a small white house with glass windows is lashed to the rocks but it sways with the wind when storms rage."

The lookout tower is equipped with telephones, binoculars, telescopes, maps and charts. It is up to Tower to keep the glasses swinging over the countryside to pick up any stray smoke, locate it on his maps and report it to the Deadwood Office which in turn reports to the ranger of the district for investigation. Tower keeps an eye out for suspicious looking characters who may be roaming around the country.

It doesn't get lonely at the lookout tower, Tower says. Many people climb the trail to see the view of the Hills. A panorama for 50-60 miles in every direction presents one of the finest views of the Hills. A good road leads to the foot of the peak and an easy trail leads to the lookout from there.

A dawn to dust vigil at 6794 feet has become a daily experience for lookouts at Custer Peak Tower located eight miles south of Lead. The tower is staffed seven days a week due to extremely dry conditions this year in the Black Hills.

A great article in the *Weekly Pioneer* dated August 8, 1940 tells of Frank Tower's experience on the lookout. The article is titled Distant Views Obtainable from Custer Peak Lookout by Lois Thrasher, "More than 120 miles north; almost 80 miles east: Harney Peak 30 miles south; the Limestone Divide 20 miles west. That's how far Frank Tower can see every day from his lofty post on the Custer Peak Lookout Station."

Tower has spent 24 summers scanning the countryside for wildfire and is still enthusiastic about the job. He looks forward to staffing the lookout each fire season.

It is a short 20-minute walk from the parking lot to the lookout station where Tower spends his days. Not that many people make the climb and many of those who do set one foot on the top step of the lookout and say they made it and then head back down the peak as quickly as they can. They seldom take time to check out the view.

Chicagoans are the best sports pointed out Tower. They sit down and really drink in the view when they reach the summit of Custer Peak.

They're in no hurry to go back down. He has little time for the fairly large class of persons who climb up solely to say they have reached the top. It can be a monotonous job he confessed, looking constantly thru his glass for signs of a fire.

The second lookout structure at Custer Peak is where Frank Tower spent most of his lookout career. He was also the only lookout to staff this lookout structure. (Courtesy U.S. Forest Service)

Frank Tower decided to retire from his lookout position in 1944 and an article in the *Black Hills Weekly* dated September 1, 1944 tells of the event planned by the U.S. Forest Service, "Farewell Party Held for Forest Service men. A farewell dinner was held at the Methodist Church Tuesday evening for several members of the Black Hills National Forest, who are leaving here or retiring.

Frank Tower was included as an honored guest, as he planned on retiring from his lookout position on Custer Peak. Tower had served as the lookout on the peak for many years. He first served at the lookout in 1911 and has spent many summers there since that time."

Carl Lindstrom of Deadwood served on Custer Peak for years, and he had staffed Terry Peak before moving to Custer Peak. An article by Anita Rochester in the *Spearfish Daily Queen City Mail* dated July 29, 1985 tells a little of Lindstrom's service as a fire lookout.

"A Black Hills native, Lindstrom enjoys his work especially the very beautiful view. Lindstrom staffs, the Custer Peak Lookout Station and is at the lookout Wednesdays through Sundays. Bernie Wanhauen, a Lead High School math instructor relieves Lindstrom as fire attendant on Monday and Tuesday."

Lightning is often the subject of many articles about fire lookouts, but it does seem the first lookouts suffered more from lightning than those in more modern eras. An article in the *Black Hills Weekly* dated May 21, 1948, describes an incident when lightning overcame a lookout on duty at Custer Peak, "Lightning played around the Custer Peak Fire Lookout on Monday night to such an extent that Jim Meyers, lookout, suffered electric shock. The station was filled with electricity for some time during the storm, and he came into Deadwood Tuesday for rest and treatment. Ranger Hugh Martin took over the station Tuesday, and it will be manned by a substitute for a few days until Meyers recovers from the mild shock."

Newspapers articles throughout the Hills often tell when the lookouts first began to staff their towers each season and details about fires and incidents during fire season. The *Black Hills Weekly* ran an article titled Fire Lookouts Up on June 3, 1964, "A fire lookout will go on duty at Custer Peak Wednesday, Jerry Martinez, Deadwood and Nemo

District said. Evelyn Sorheim, Lead, will be on duty for the season. A former resident of Newcastle, Wyoming, she has been a lookout on Mount Pisgah, near Newcastle, for the past three years. The fire lookout station on Terry Peak also is officially open with John Sloss, Deadwood, on duty."

Current Custer Peak Fire Lookout. (Courtesy U.S. Forest Service)

Original cabin and lookout at Cement Ridge.
(Courtesy U.S. Forest Service)

Second Cement Ridge Lookout. (Courtesy U.S. Forest Service)

The original Cement Ridge log cabin and lookout evolved between 1911 and 1913. In 1921 the second lookout sitting to the left of the log cabin in photo was built. The CCCs completed the final lookout structure in 1941 still serving on the ridge for the detection of forest fires.

Newspapers in the area reported on the activities at Cement Ridge during the early years. The *Crook County Monitor* dated July 19, 1912, tells about the person staffing the lookout, "D.L. Van Meter, lookout for the Forest Service at Cement Ridge was in the city Tuesday. He says when last seen the elk turned loose on the headwaters of Sand Creek last spring were doing fine."

In January of 1913, the *Monitor* told about construction at the lookout site, "A forest guard was stationed at Cement Ridge Lookout Station where a cabin has been built, connected by Forest Service phone with the ranger's headquarters and the Supervisor's office. This lookout discovered 13 of the 15 fires that occurred during the summer."

Current Lookout Station atop Cement Ridge built in 1940.
(Courtesy U.S. Forest Service)

The Black Hills National Forest was one of the first in the nation to use the Osborne Fire-Finder. The *Deadwood-Pioneer Times* presented an article on the new device in June 12, 1918. "A new and improved method of locating fires is being installed at the Custer Peak and Cement Ridge Lookout Stations of the Black Hills National Forest. The accurate location of a column of smoke rising from a timbered country 10 to 30 miles distant from the lookout is a difficult matter unless the smoke can be reported simultaneously from two or more observation points, the introduction of the Osborne Fire-Finder."

Every lookout tower is equipped with an Osborne Fire-Finder, and it is the main tool the fire lookout uses. The fire-finder is truly nothing but a giant compass which helps to create a legal description of the fire and shows its direction from the lookout tower which is called the azimuth.

By sighting on a fire, the degree readings running around the outside of the fire finder corresponds with township, range and quarter section on the map. A good legal description of the location of the fire helps fire fighters to mobilize more quickly without wasting time searching for the fire.

Osborne Fire-Finder. (Courtesy Dixie Boyle)

Before the construction of lookout towers, smoke chasers used an alidade and protractor in the same way to pinpoint a fire. All they had to do was find a suitable tree stump in the forest where they could see the fire and line it up on their map.

The Osborne Fire-Finder was created by a Forest Service employee named William Osborne from the Mt. Hood National Forest in Oregon in 1911. The instrument is accurate down to one-sixtieth of a degree. Osborne improved the fire-finder in the 1930s. The current fire-finder used in fire towers throughout the country is half the size of those used during Osborne's time. The fire-finder is located in the center of every lookout station, so the lookout can easily swing it around to the degree readings when reporting a wildfire.

Tom Sawyer was the first lookout to drive a vehicle to the Cement Ridge lookout site. The slope to the lookout was so steep that he had to place a sack of potatoes behind the back tires while he cleared brush in front of the vehicle. In this way he was able to slowly inch toward the lookout. He remained at the site the remainder of fire season, and the U.S. Forest Service packed in water and supplies by mule train.

According to the *Deadwood Pioneer-Times* dated December 30, 1958, Vernon Tollefson staffed the Cement Ridge Lookout for fifteen years. He came to the area from Sioux Falls and worked with the Civilian Conservation Corps. He served as mess sergeant with the army before entering the U.S. Forest Service. He was at Nemo for two years and at Roubaix for the same length of time. In 1958 he transferred to the lookout on Terry Peak. The article went on to tell how he would live at the new recreation dwelling at Sheridan Lake and was joined by his family during the summer months.

Tollefson, an ardent conservationist, was awarded the annual Conservation Award of the Lead Rod and Gun Club. Mrs. Tollefson was employed as a teacher. The couple had four children, Jorand 15, Gary 14, Karen 12 and Selene 11, who attended the public schools in Lead when not living with their father at the fire tower.

The *Queen City Mail* dated July 23, 1975 had an interesting article titled: Local Girl is mountain top Sentinel. The article tells of Jane Russell who was the fire lookout on Cement Ridge in 1975, "On a high hill 27 miles from Spearfish, a fire lookout tower stands in the lonely terrain of the Northern Black Hills. It is beautiful ponderosa pine country here, but the frightening danger of forest fire haunts its fragile beauty. Watching over this domain from the Cement Ridge Tower is fire lookout Jane Russell."

The Black Hills has active fire seasons. The Cement Ridge Lookout spotted ten of the forest fires last year. It is Russell's job from June to November to spot fires from her lookout post.

It is lonely work covering this district—the responsibility of twenty square miles of land rests on her ability to notice fires, accurately locate them and report them quickly. Every 15 minutes Jane makes her rounds, checking in each direction for signs of forest fires.

Few visitors make it up the rough gravel road to the tower, but they are rewarded with an incomparable view of these forest covered Hills. On a clear day one can see as far as the Big Horn Mountains 175 miles away.

Jane, who graduated this May from the University of New Mexico with a degree in biology and psychology, will be returning there this fall to attend graduate school. But for now, watching this land for threats to its growing life is her job.

The *Queen City Mail* dated August 10, 1983 tells of an Iowa couple who staffed Cement Ridge in 1983, "Larry and Marion LaBeune of Hornick, Iowa, are spending the summer at the top of Cement Ridge Lookout Tower, 11 miles southwest of Spearfish. The Iowa couple is serving as Forest Service volunteers.

According to Pete Johnston district ranger, this is the first year the lookout has been staffed with volunteers. Their job says Johnston, is to provide visitors with information and also be on the lookout for fires.

In fact, the couple spotted a wildfire the first day they were in the tower and have been doing an excellent job ever since said Johnston. The LaBeunes have also spent several days cleaning, painting and performing minor maintenance to the tower. The couple lives in Spearfish but spend the day in the tower. They pretty much accepted the position in the blind, though there were quite a few telephone conversations, said Glenn Jackson, also with the U.S. Forest Service.

LaBeune retired as a station agent for the Milwaukee Railroad after more than 34 years. He has also served as a volunteer fireman since 1965 in Hornick.

The couple spends their time off fishing, shopping, attending auction sales and touring the Hills. Although they enjoy their time off, they are happy to return to the cooler temperatures at the tower."

The first lookout structure on Elk Mountain was erected in the1930s and later used on Rankin Ridge in the late 1950s. (Courtesy U.S. Forest Service)

Elk Mountain Fire Lookout in 1942. (Courtesy U.S. Forest Service)

Two steel, Aermotor towers were erected on both Elk Mountain and Summit Ridge in 1940. Built near the end of the Great Depression, the lookouts were part of the last great spurt of Civilian Conservation Corps lookout construction before the start of World War II. They are identical in appearance and dimensions and built by Aermotor, a well-known company in Chicago responsible for building the utilitarian type lookouts of the era.

In 2001, the Elk Mountain Fire forever changed the landscape around the fire tower. The *Rapid City Journal* dated August 6, 2001 tells of the fire destroying the lookout site, "The Elk Mountain Fire burned right up to the steel base of the Elk Mountain Lookout Tower. It destroyed the adjoining cabin and its contents."

The Elk Mountain Fire roared over the top of the Elk Mountain Range and burned 13,195 acres as well as the lookout cabin and outhouse and most of the trees that once surrounded the tower. The U.S. Forest Service began replanting ponderosa pine trees in the area in 2005.

The fire destroyed all the old growth ponderosa pine trees once found throughout the mountain range and surrounding the Elk Mountain Lookout Tower. The fire changed the atmosphere at the lookout but it has retained its own beauty and continues its service as a fire lookout.

An article in Newcastle's *News-Letter Journal* dated July 6, 1939 tells of the new Elk Mountain Lookout tower, "Elk Mountain Lookout Tower, recently completely by the U.S. Forest Service can easily be seen from Highway 16 as you go east from Newcastle, looming up on the extreme north end of the mountain.

Earl Wilkinson of Pleasant Valley is maintaining a constant vigilance from this point and notices any smoke sighted, which tell him there is a fire running loose and reports its location promptly to the U.S. Forest Service at the fire dispatching office at Custer.

A woman named Minnie Cooper worked on this lookout for sixteen years. The first few years she had the job she rode to the lookout on horseback and packed in her supplies for the fire season. According to the log book of 1959, the lookouts worked from April through November unless it snowed.

Minnie brought canned supplies and even a flock of chickens to the mountaintop for the summer. She was an amazingly dedicated lookout, as she went up into the tower on her own time and even slept in a narrow cot she had cut down to fit in the lookout tower so she could track lightning during the evening hours.

There were only a few primitive roads in the area in 1943 when Minnie first started working Elk Mountain Lookout. She blazed a trail to the lookout up the east side of the range and hiked back and forth until a road was constructed to the site.

I wonder if Minnie felt sad about having to leave the mountaintop at the end of fire season, I just read the last entry she wrote in the logbook at the end of the 1959 lookout season, "Closing the lookout and am afraid this might have to be my last year." She must have already known she had cancer and would not be returning to Elk Mountain, and I am sure it was a sad time for her. She passed away that winter and is buried in the Custer, South Dakota Cemetery.

An article in the *Rapid City Journal* dated June 29, 1952 gives a little more insight into the work Minnie Cooper performed at the Elk Mountain Fire Tower, "Mrs. Cooper's services are invaluable during a fire. She is also the Elk Mountain Ranger District fire dispatcher. She orders men, tankers and other equipment and supplies sent to the fire according to the needs of the fire boss. She relays orders and requests for men and materials."

According to the article, she constantly sends in reports on the progress of the fire and is on 24-hour duty. During the day she sends and receives more than twenty calls and transmits her messages with efficiency in a clear voice.

On her own time, she cooks her meals, does her laundry and cuts fire wood for her cook stove. Most summers she keeps about 50 chickens on the mountain, which provides her with eggs and fresh meat. Mrs. Cooper's hobbies are crocheting, reading and writing. She has a wide circle of friends and writes many letters.

Minnie Cooper owns a home in Dewey, about 20 miles from Elk Mountain, and during the winter she makes her home there. She was born in Crawford, Nebraska.

Other lookouts and alternates in the Harney National Forest are George and Belle Sturn, Bear Mountain; Galen and Effie McCain, Boulder Hill; Sid and Ann Manary, Cicero Peak; Myron and David Hazeltine, Harney Peak; Ella and Charles Scott, Mount Pisgah, Chester Williams, Parker Peak, and Frank and Mabel Lanouette, Summit Ridge.

Another interesting article in the *Rapid City Journal* dated September 19, 1967 tells of the lookout experience of Frances Reman who served on Elk Mountain in the 1960s. Before accepting the job as the primary lookout on Elk Mountain, Frances had served as a part-time relief lookout. She enjoyed the experience so much that when the article was written she had been spotting fires at the Elk Mountain Lookout for five years.

She explained the type of people who were the most successful working alone in an isolated fire tower, "A person has to enjoy their own company. They need to enjoy living alone and know how to entertain themselves." During her off-duty hours she painted with oils, read books and wrote poetry.

When asked about the ratio of men to women and the future of the Forest Service she replied, "About one half of lookout personnel are men. Fewer towers are needed nowadays than in years gone by because we have such good air coverage. Pilots have an advantage over lookouts as they can spot smaller fires." The Black Hills National Forest must have agreed with Reman, as lookouts soon began closing throughout the Black Hills.

Summit Ridge Lookout Cabin is identical to one lost during the Elk Mountain Fire. (Courtesy U.S. Forest Service)

In March of 1907 President Theodore Roosevelt created by presidential proclamation the Bearlodge National Forest with headquarters in Sundance. The following year the name was changed to the Sundance National Forest and included all portions of the forest in Wyoming. In 1915, the Sundance National Forest merged with the Black Hills National Forest.

In 1938 the CCCs built the original fire lookout structure on Warren Peaks, a half mile west of the location of the present lookout tower. The wooden tower was used for twenty years. Maurice Classick staffed Warren Peak after moving to the area to work with the CCCs in 1934. He was on the crew that built the original wooden tower, as well as on the crew that tore it down. He was also part of the crew in 1960 that helped to construct the steel tower that now resides on the peak.

Original Fire Lookout on Warren Peak. (Courtesy U.S. Forest Service)

The *Weekly Pioneer-Times* newspaper dated March 9, 1939 provides information about the building of the original fire tower on Warren Peaks. "In November, work was started on a wooden lookout cabin. Due to weather conditions the job could not be completed in 1938 and work was discontinued December 1. As soon as the forest road is open in April this year, the building will be rushed to completion in order to have it ready for the 1939 fire season."

The new lookout is fourteen feet square and consists of one room that will serve as the lookout station and living quarters for the lookout on duty. The lookout is glass enclosed and surrounded by a three-foot catwalk

The first lookout to work the new structure was Lyman Ellsbury, the son of Mert Ellsbury at Aladdin. Lyman is a forestry graduate of Fort Collins agricultural college and has had other work in the service, coming here from the experimental station at Fort Collins. He was recently married to a Fort Collins girl.

Another article in the *Weekly Pioneer Times* dated August 10, 1939 describes how dangerous lightning on these peaks could really be at times, "While talking over the telephone at the new lookout station on Warren Peaks Monday, Ranger T.R. Cochran was struck by a bolt of lightning that traveled down the telephone line. He was knocked over backwards down the slope and suffered painful bruises about one knee, ankle and foot. Just how long he was unconscious is not known."

Maurice Classick would take over the lookout duties in 1941 as described in the *Deadwood Pioneer Times* on June 7, 1941, "Mr. and Mrs. Maurice Classick, and daughter, Maurine, left this week for Sundance where they will make their future home. Mr. Classick will be fire lookout for the Black Hills National Forest at the lookout on Warren Peak near Sundance."

Warren Peak overlooks the Powder River Basin country to the west and the Big Horn Mountains where the basin ends on the horizon. To the north is the Custer National Forest in Montana and to the east is the rest of the Black Hills National Forest and the prairies of South

Dakota. The endless Wyoming plains are to the south between the Bearlodge Mountains and Laramie Peak on the Medicine Bow National Forest with Thunder Basin National Grasslands in between.

Bull Hill, Ellsbury and Taylor Divides, Blacktail Creek, Stony Point, Sheep Mountain, Inyan Kara Mountain and Devils Tower. The community of Sundance is eight miles from the lookout and has a population of a little over a thousand people. It really is a small, picturesque community.

My journal entry dated August 15, 1992 describes one of the most unusual fires I reported during my time on Warren Peak, "My supervisor sent me up to work the lookout today as it has not rained in a couple weeks and we had a lightning storm last night. As soon as I arrived at the fire tower, I picked up two snags burning along the north end, but they were almost out by the time crews arrived on them.

This afternoon a bolt of lightning hit east of the lookout on Richardson Ridge and almost immediately a thin, column of smoke came up. I quickly called in the fire and crews found it in a short time. Upon their arrival they requested butchering knives in a joking manner over the radio. When I hesitated to relay their message, they called back with laughter in their voices as they described two cows under the tree hit by lightning. The cows were dead of course with their feet touching. Everyone had a good laugh over those cows, except for the rancher who owned them. He came up to the lookout a few days later wanting directions to the location of their bodies. That was quite the lightning strike apparently."

It is always a difficult decision to decide to leave a lookout job, and of all the lookouts I worked during my years with the Black Hills National Forest, Warren Peak is the fire lookout I miss the most. My parents needed help with the ranch back in New Mexico so I headed back home at the end of fire season in 1999 with a heavy heart. I wrote, "Today is my last day on Warren Peak. The lump in my throat has threatened to burst all day, as I will really miss the view from my mountain peak. The Bearlodge Mountains and their endless view of the Great Plains will walk in my soul forever. It is close to impossible to say goodbye. Hopefully I will make it back one day."

The Sioux and Cheyenne roamed between the Bearlodge Mountains and the Powder River Basin country for over a century before the Custer Expedition discovered gold in 1874. General George Armstrong Custer camped near the base of Inyan Kara Mountain and buried two of his troopers there. Even the Sundance Kid of the Hole- in- the- Wall Gang is part of the history. He gained his alias when he spent time in the Sundance Jail for stealing a horse, gun and saddle from a rancher near Aladdin.

Devils Tower and Sundance Mountain help to surround the Bearlodge Mountains. The Plains tribes used the Vore Buffalo Jump near Beulah to run buffalo over the edge to their deaths in order to procure their winter food supply. Sand Creek near Beulah is where Teddy Roosevelt took his son to camp, fish and experience the American frontier before it was gone.

The mountain man Jedidiah Smith encountered a grizzly bear in Crook County while passing through on his way to Yellowstone. Dinosaur remains have been uncovered throughout the region. That pioneer spirit vibrates throughout the landscape and on the faces of the people, and they share a sense of independence I have never seen anywhere else. I will always miss this magical landscape and its history.

The lookouts in the Black Hills have always been tourist attractions. An article in Newcastle's *News Letter Journal* dated May 11, 1944 tells of the decrease in visitors due to World War II, "All the hundreds and thousands of visitors who puff their way to inaccessible lookouts have one favorite question: Don't you get lonesome up here all alone? This year with tires and gas on the missing side and even shoes rationed, they won't be here to ask, and for the first time, they might be right."

Lookout personnel for the 1944 season in the Black Hills were: Maurice Classick on Warren Peak in the Bearlodge, Frank Tower was back at his old post on Custer Peak, Verne Tollefson staffed the Cement Ridge Lookout, Frank Kaump was at Flag Mountain and Raymond Hall worked at Seth Bullock.

The *Casper-Star Tribune* dated October 24, 1940 shows the major fire season the Black Hills can have from time to time, "More than fifty fires were reported for the season in the Warren Peak area of the Black

Hills National Forest in northeast Wyoming. Ben Mahoney, lookout located at the Warren Peak station, reported 56 fires for the entire seaon, of which 36 required action by the United States Forest Service."

The view from Warren Peak is amazing and is definitely a main lookout point for the Black Hills National Forest. Another article in the *Casper-Star Tribune* dated August 29, 1939 tells of that endless view, "One of the most striking views afforded in the state is that seen from the Warren Peak Lookout tower recently completed. Portions of Wyoming, South Dakota and Montana can be viewed from the peak on clear days, with evening sunsets of the Big Horns in bold relief. Devils Tower and the Missouri Buttes may also be seen from the station. The tower is for fire prevention and Mr. and Mrs. Lyman Ellsbury are occupying the living quarters there."

A lookout pair named Classick worked the lookout site on Warren Peak possibly the longest of any lookouts stationed on the peak. An article in the *Rapid City Journal* dated August 21, 1946 tells of Mr. and Mrs. Classick working the tower, "Mr. and Mrs. M.J. Classick's Black Hills home is 6700 feet above sea level. They live in a 16 X 16 foot glass-enclosed, government house atop Warren Peak from April until snow covers the timbered area they observe in sufficient depth to eliminate the threat of forest fires. The rest of the time their residence is Sundance."

Maurice Classick was the primary lookout on Warren Peak, but his wife also served as the lookout when her husband was fighting fires in the area. She enjoyed lookout duty. She liked being alone and felt cooped up in her house in Sundance. She loved the open spaces surrounding the lookout tower.

Karen Maloy, a native of Panama City in the Florida Panhandle, staffed Warren Peak for eleven years. While attending Black Hills State University, she applied for work as a fire lookout at the Cement Ridge Lookout Site. The lookout was not staffed during these years and her application was forwarded to the Bearlodge Ranger District where she was offered Warren Peak Lookout.

Karen staffed Warren Peak from 2001 through the 2007 fire season when she was called back to Florida to help with family matters. Five years later, she returned to lookout duty on Warren Peak and staffed the site through the 2016 fire season. In 2017 she moved to eastern Oregon where she has staffed Indian Rock Lookout in the Malheur National Forest near John Day ever since.

Karen began her career as a fire lookout in Idaho's Payette National Forest on Indian Mountain Fire Lookout. She soon discovered lookout duty was her line of work and recently completed her twentieth year as a fire lookout. As of the publication of this book, she has no plans of retiring soon.

Karen, as lookouts before her, loved Warren Peak and its view of the Great Plains and Black Hills. But, she decided to move to Oregon and replied when asked about her reasons, "I really enjoyed Warren Peak and all the folks there, but it got too crazy with three thousand or more visitors each summer plus lots of fire activity at the same time. I needed a station with fewer visitors."

She not only worked as a fire lookout during her years with the Black Hills NF, but since she has a degree in forestry she also helped with forestry projects. She helped with RX Burns and staffed Cement Ridge and Custer Peak for short fire assignments.

Fire Lookouts in the Black Hills can get busy during the summer months and dealing with elevated fire activity and large groups of visitors do not always mix well. Recently the Black Hills National Forest closed their lookouts to visitors. In most cases, visitors can climb the stairs and walk around the lookout site but not enter the tower.

Warren Peak is normally an active fire lookout with the constant ignition of fires during fire season. Karen tells of her busiest day on Warren Peak, "The day started with a call from my supervisor at 3:00 one morning. He said there had been over 5,000 lightning strikes. County crews were already fighting multiple fires and to head to the lookout tower as soon as possible. When I climbed the lookout stairs at dawn, I saw multiple fires. Before the day ended, I had reported eighteen fires and those were only the ones I could see. The whole county was literally on fire."

Karen's present lookout Indian Rock does not receive the visitation she had at Warren Peak. Her site requires a quarter mile hike to the tower which discourages some people. She receives between 150 and 200 visitors a summer, quite a decrease from Warren Peak.

The way she works with other lookout towers has changed since relocating to Oregon Karen pointed out, "I went from having no other tower to work with to working with multiple towers on different forests. My tower sits at the northeast edge of the Malheur National Forest and butts up against the Wallowa-Whiteman and Umatilla National Forests, so four towers can work together if needed."

I did not live in the tower at Warren Peak as most of the lookouts drive back and forth to their lookout sites. In Oregon all the lookouts live in their towers, as the roads are rough and distances too far to drive back and forth. This past summer our lookout sites were closed for almost a month due to wildfire activity so only had around a hundred visitors and a lot of them were hunters.

Warren Peak Fire Lookout and the Northern Lights in the background. (Courtesy David M. Porter Photography)

Current Warren Peak. (Courtesy Dixie Boyle)

Original wooden tower at Mt. Coolidge. (Courtesy Custer State Park)

Current Mt. Coolidge Fire Lookout. (Courtesy Custer State Park)

The Daily Deadwood Pioneer Times dated June 16, 1928 explains the building of the original lookout on Mt. Coolidge, "Theodore Shoemaker, State Park forester, states that the long-contemplated tower on Mt. Coolidge is being built. It will be 60 feet square at the top. Four huge logs, each 60 feet in length, 20 inches in diameter at the base and 12 inches in diameter at the top will form the corner pieces to which the side logs will be attached. The entire structure will be built of logs. They are hauled to the top of Mt. Coolidge with trucks, the road being in very fair condition. On the very top will be a room ten feet square, where the lookout can use if he desires. A stairway will be constructed from the lower floor to the room above."

Another article in the *Rapid City Journal* dated August 9, 1941 explains the cost and location of the fire lookout, "The new lookout atop Mt. Coolidge in Custer State Park has been completed at a cost of $15,000 commissioner Earl Hammerquist of the school and public lands department said today.

An ample parking space and terraced landscape surrounds the observation tower. It has living quarters for Clarence Mann fire prevention worker in charge of the lookout area.

Abandonment of the Mt. Coolidge CCC Camp made fire prevention the responsibility of the school and public lands department, Hammerquist said. Other state and national agencies are cooperating to eliminate fire hazards and fire departments and private citizens of nearby towns are organized in preparation for any eventuality."

An early lookout on Mt. Coolidge was a man named Frank Walsh as described in the *Weekly Pioneer Times* in June of 1933, "Frank Walsh, who grew up in Custer County, was named lookout for Mt. Coolidge this season on Wednesday. The appointment was made by Ben Strool, state commissioner of public lands in charge of the state forest interests.

Walsh has lived all of his life in the shadow of Mt. Coolidge and knows the points of local history and geography that will be of interest to visitors. He is a practical man in the woods, and makes a good man for lookout at the ranger station there. He moved out to the lookout headquarters Wednesday night."

Gail Duncan Herbert staffed Mt. Coolidge and other towers throughout the Black Hills for a total of 35 years before retiring in 1981. While working fire towers, Gail spent her free time studying law and hoped she passed the bar exam. She stated, "I don't think I will practice law. It's just a personal goal."

Gail began her career as a fire lookout in 1946 when she scanned for fires from an old, wooden tower on Parker Peak between Hot Springs and Edgemont. In 1953 she moved to Mt. Coolidge. It was from this vantage point she dispatched crews from the Southern Black Hills to a wildfire that threatened Deadwood, 100 miles to the north. It was September 8, 1959.

She told about the fire in an interview, "You could see that smoke for miles and miles. I can still shut my eyes and see it. It was a madhouse. I never stopped talking on the radio for 48 hours straight." She received a commendation from then Governor Ralph Herseth for her work.

Gail left Mt. Coolidge in 1966 after spending thirteen years staffing the site. She went on to work at towers on Cicero Peak, Harney Peak, Rankin Ridge, Bear Mountain and Elk Mountain.

Post card of Mt. Coolidge. (Courtesy author's collection)

The present structure at Mt. Coolidge was erected by the CCCs in 1939. The site has also been known as Sheep Mountain and Lookout Mountain. From the beginning, the site was popular with visitors. The *Deadwood-Pioneer* tells about the crowds in an article dated July 3, 1929, "More than 200 persons in automobiles, a record for the season, drove up to Mt. Coolidge Sunday to enjoy the scenic panorama," S. Hazelton in charge of the lookout said.

The original mountain was known as Sheep Mountain to old-timers in the area. In 1923 a log cabin and caretaker's structure were built and the mountain named Lookout Mountain. In 1927 the site was renamed Mt. Coolidge and in 1939 the Civilian Conservation Corp built a stone lookout and caretaker's quarters. The lookout is located ten miles south of Mt. Rushmore.

An interesting article was found in the *Deadwood-Pioneer Times* dated April 16, 1927, "A log tower is to be built on Lookout Mountain this spring, superintendent Dennison of the state park has announced that will appeal strongly to many people who have climbed the sound but spindly looking iron tower that has graced the peak for years. The man halfway up that swaying trestle has much to think about on a windy day. Darned if I go down, because that would look like cold feet, but darned if he wants to go up because the thing wobbles so. A substantial log tower, produced on the spot, would have been welcomed by many a man in nearly every recent summer."

Information on back of postcard: Mount Coolidge, formerly called Sheep Mountain, was renamed after the visit of President Calvin Coolidge to the Black Hills in 1927. A good auto route leads to the top of the mountain, altitude 6400 feet, from where a vista unequaled in beauty is attainable. From a fire tower, 75 feet high, the vigilance of forest rangers guards against devastating fires and protects mountain timber.

Another article in the *Queen City Mail* dated October 8, 1930 tells of the wonderful view from the Mt. Coolidge Lookout Tower, "It is claimed that the lookout on Mt. Coolidge cannot only view a large tract of the Black Hills from his door yard, but with a field glass can watch work on Rushmore mountain, and get a view of the Badlands, all without leaving home."

Article in *Rapid City Journal* dated July 22, 1939, "A towering Mt. Coolidge in the state park is a primary lookout station and manned during the entire season. Clarence Mann is on duty. Living quarters and a concession stand are located at the foot of the tower."

BLACK HILLS FIRE LOOKOUTS
NO LONGER USED BUT STILL STANDING

There are seven fire lookouts no longer used for the detection of forest fires that remain standing throughout the Black Hills National Forest. One of the lookouts overlooks Pactola Reservoir and is maintained by the U.S. Forest Service. The lookout is used to house radio equipment as well as the repeater. The site was named after Seth Bullock, an early sheriff and supervisor of the Black Hills National Forest.

An article in the *Rapid City Journal* on December 7, 1938 explains the naming of the lookout site and a little history of Lawrence County, "Naming of the lookout for the late Captain Bullock ties in with the custom of retaining all the historical flavor of the Black Hills that it is possible to do. Bullock was the first sheriff of Lawrence County and identified as being in the cattle business. He owned several ranches on the Belle Fourche River, and is credited with raising the first alfalfa grown in South Dakota. He was a personal friend of Teddy Roosevelt and received his appointment as supervisor through him."

The article goes on to tell about Bullock and the building of the lookout in his name, "Seth Bullock, first supervisor, of the Black Hills National Forest and prominent in early Black Hills history, will be honored by a new lookout station to be built near Pactola, the Seth Bullock Lookout."

The first tower on Seth Bullock was a 30-foot-high log structure. A 16 x 16-foot observatory was located at the top for the observation of forest fire. The rocky pinnacle where the lookout resides is so steep that a place big enough for the lookout had to be blasted off the rocks with dynamite.

According to the *Rapid City Journal* in September of 1966, the third and final lookout erected at the lookout site was moved from the Pisgah Lookout site east of Newcastle, Wyoming. The article stated, "The skyline at Pactola is due a slight change when a new Seth Bullock Lookout rises on the rock in the foreground and the wooden structure, date 1939, comes down. Hanna & Hanna Construction Company,

Desoto, Texas, is moving the Pisgah Mountain Lookout to Seth Bullock. With an added 13 feet, the Pisgah Lookout will rise to 67 feet atop the 6,000-foot Seth Bullock site by October 8." The old Pisgah Lookout has remained there ever since.

The first lookouts also took extensive weather readings to determine the fire danger. An article in the *Lead Daily Call* dated June 6, 1948 by Camille Yuill titled No Fire Escapes Lookout's Eyes tells of this practice no longer done by present day lookouts. "A man who lives in a glass house, 5509 feet above sea level, is not in much danger of having stones thrown at him but Roy Ketchum faces other hazards.

From May until the end of the forest fire season, he is perched in his tower on Seth Bullock Lookout. The winds blow all the time, and the pyrotechnic display that comes frequently from the lightning storms keeps him on the alert most of the time."

The article describes the inside of the lookout tower. There was a stove, bed, table, two or three chairs, radio, direction finder, maps and telephone. The direction finder was located in the middle of the room and maps with pointers and charts were also available to help when reporting a fire.

Another important piece of equipment was the fire hazard chart by which he determines the fire danger. Based on temperatures, winds, humidity, length of time since last rain, conditions of annual plants and fuel moisture he is able to calculate the fire danger. When it gets above 75, he and everyone else on the forest are on the lookout for fire. The readings are taken several times daily at each of the lookouts and reported to the office in Deadwood by three pm each day.

Ketchum served on the lookout for a decade. When he was not on fire duty, he operated a small farm near Pactola and made cabinets and did carpentry work.

Photo shows current and second Seth Bullock Lookout in the background.
(Courtesy U.S. Forest Service)

The second Seth Bullock Lookout was blown up with dynamite and demolished in 1975. (Courtesy U.S. Forest Service)

Summit Ridge Fire Lookout has not been staffed since 1972 when the Elk Mountain District decided to downsize their fire lookout stations. The tower on Summit Ridge is used as a secondary lookout.

Original Summit Ridge Fire Lookout later named the Moon Tower.
(Courtesy Ed Mason)

Summit Ridge Lookout began its history in 1935 when a Civilian Conservation Crew led by Ed Mason erected a wooden lookout tower on the site. The crew initially built the lookout on private land in Wyoming one half mile west of its present location. Upon realizing their mistake, they moved the lookout by balancing it on chains between two small tractors.

The wooden lookout built by Ed Mason's crew is no longer standing and was only used at the Summit Ridge Lookout site for five years before the present steel tower was erected. In 1940, the lookout structure was moved to another high ridge known as Fairy Gates south of Moon Campground and renamed the Moon Tower. The lookout was used as a secondary lookout for twenty years before being cut down with chainsaws and partially buried where it stood.

Moving Summit Ridge Fire Lookout. (Courtesy Ed Mason)

Burning, burying or moving were often the fates of the unused fire lookouts starting in the 1970s throughout the nation's forests. The construction boom of the CCC era was becoming a liability or so the U.S. Forest Service thought at the time.

Although a secondary lookout, Summit Ridge was an important relay station during fires. As the U.S. Forest Service downsized in the 1970s, Summit Ridge would be another casualty of lookout reduction in the Black Hills. Elk Mountain had always been the primary lookout, and it was felt Summit Ridge was not needed as in the past. The lookout site is used as a secondary lookout after lightning storms and when looking for a fire but was otherwise left unstaffed. The site has become a popular rental for the U.S. Forest Service.

The lookout tower is still used on occasion for the detection of forest fires and the CCC cabin nearby is rented out to the public when weather permits. As all lookout rentals the site is popular and reservations should be made a year in advance.

Summit Ridge LO shortly after Construction in 1940.
(Courtesy U.S. Forest Service)

The logs in the foreground are laid out in preparation to build the log cabin where the lookout would live while on duty. Since the lookouts as well as the log cabins were identical for the Elk Mountain and Summit Ridge Lookout sites, the logs intended for Elk Mountain were transported to Summit Ridge and Summit Ridge's logs to Elk Mountain. It did not seem to make much difference in the end though.

The *News-Letter Journal* dated July 27, 1950 points out a lookout couple from Custer, South Dakota who staffed the Summit Ridge site for several years, "The position at Summit Ridge in the extreme northwest corner of Custer County, is jointly held by Mr. and Mrs. Frank Lanouette, who have for several years shared the responsibility of spotting smoke in the high hazard area in that corner of the forest. Mr. and Mrs. Lanouette find time to entertain their six children and numerous grandchildren who keep things lively by frequent visits to the two-room cabin high up on Summit Ridge."

Summit Ridge Lookout. (Courtesy U.S. Forest Service)

Terry Peak Fire Lookout. (Courtesy U.S. Forest Service)

Terry Peak, one of the highest lookouts in the Black Hills is no longer in service for the detection of forest fires. The cab has been removed from the peak and only a viewing platform remains. The lookout site has not been used for the detection of forest fires since the 1970s when many towers in the Hills were shut down. The location remains popular with tourists and locals and is used as a visitor center.

Lead Daily Call dated September 1, 1949, "Construction of a new fire lookout on top of Terry Peak, the second highest mountain in the Black Hills, is expected to start soon, C.C. Averill, supervisor of the Black Hills National Forest said today." The fire lookout would not be completed until the following year.

The lookout's construction was delayed by the weather often a major issue in the Black Hills. An article in the *Lead Daily Call* dated April 11, 1950 tells of the construction of the lookout tower, "Crews of the Black Hills National Forest are clearing out the road to the top of Terry Peak, preparatory to constructing a fire lookout station, C.C. Averill, supervisor said this morning."

The men are encountering eight-foot drifts, he said, and it will take several days to get the road open so that materials can be taken to the top of the mountain. The lookout will be the second highest in the Black Hills, with the one on Harney Peak in first place. It will be constructed at the very top of the peak. Concrete foundations for the post were set last fall.

The lookout will be a 14 x 14-foot glass enclosed cab on a rock understructure. The living quarters will be in the understructure. It will be the only fire lookout in the Black Hills to have electricity. The outlets will provide for electric stove, refrigerator and other equipment to make living during the fire season more comfortable for the lookout, Averill commented.

By the 1950s, the lookout site started to receive more visitors than it could adequately handle and still serve its main duty as a fire lookout. An article in the *Black Hills Weekly* dated July 10, 1963 by Wynnifred Lindstorm tells how the U.S. Forest Service dealt with the problem, "A view that money can't buy, and all for free, is one of the reasons that the lookout tower at Terry Peak has a third floor.

The United States Forest Service site is one of the most popular tourist attractions in the Northern Black Hills. In fact, it has become so popular that the Forest Service had to do something about it."

And so last year they solved the problem of the tourist versus fire suppression by separating the two. And as a result, the lookout room was put on stilts and a special room for visitors was built between it and the lookout's bachelor quarters on the first floor."

The three-story structure works well when it is loaded with tourists and busy with fire activity at the same time. Last year over 65,000 visitors were tallied at the site. Each year the number of visitors seemed to increase.

When the Black Hills National Forest downsized their fire towers in the 1970s, Terry Peak was another lookout closed. An article in the *Black Hills Weekly* dated October 11, 1978 explains what the Forest Service did with the lookout site, "The U.S. Forest Service Fire Lookout tower on top of Terry Peak is in the final stages of a face-lifting but its days as a fire spotting station are over.

When remodeling work is completed, it will be strictly a vantage point for tourists and local visitors to view a scenic panorama of the Northern Black Hills. Only a maintenance man will be on duty to keep snow shoveled from the visitor viewing deck and sidewalks, keep an eye on the Forest Service radio equipment and possibly do some public relations work with the tourists."

In 1973 the tower ceased to be used as a fire lookout but continued to draw thousands of visitors every year, including many that rode the chair lift to the top for a better view of the Black Hills.

Rufus Pilcher and his Brother Warren Glassing
and Plotting Forest Fires in 1911. (Courtesy U.S. Forest Service)

The first lookout in the Black Hills was established on Harney Peak in 1911. The site would be considered primitive by today's standards. Rufus Pilcer was the first lookout to staff the site, and he rode to the top on horseback with his gear and fire finding equipment. His brother Warren accompanied him on his first trip to establish the lookout station.

They lived in a canvas tent and used a wooden crate with an alidade to determine direction and distance in reporting a fire. The following morning when Pilcher looked out of his tent, he saw the first forest fire reported from a fire lookout in the Black Hills. Flashing mirror signals in Morse code were used to alert crews who were waiting and watching in the valleys below.

Pilcher was born in 1887 and attended schools in Custer before graduating and earning a degree at the University of Nebraska. Afterwards he returned to the Black Hills and landed a job as the superintendent at Wind Cave National Park for a year before accepting a position with the U.S. Forest Service. He only staffed Harney Peak for one year, and spent his other four years with the agency at Hardy Guard Station and was on the first mapping crew for the Black Hills National Forest.

He enlisted in the U.S. Cavalry in 1917 and was soon commissioned to work in the aviation section of the Signal Corps and flew and taught aerial gunnery. Later, he would become a commercial pilot. When he returned to active duty he served as flier and Army Air Corps leader in England during World War II.

In later years, he moved to Riverton, California and worked as the manager of the Riverton County Hospital and as a veteran's administration hospital official until he moved to Camino for full retirement in 1965. He was eighty-four years old when he passed away leaving behind a full and interesting life.

Interior of Harney Peak in 1925 and P.L. Ginter serving as fire lookout on the peak. In August of 2016 the name Harney Peak was officially changed to Black Elk Peak after the Sioux medicine man and warrior who used Harney Peak as a spiritual area as did members of the Sioux tribe.
(Courtesy U.S. Forest Service)

Harney/Black Elk Peak was designed by architect Ellis Groben. He produced blue prints and concepts for U.S. Forest Service structures throughout the United States. His draftsman Ed Hamilton detailed these sketches further and helped the different forests to implement this type of design.

Groben grew up in Philadelphia, Pennsylvania and attended the University of Pennsylvania for his under graduate degree in architectural training. After receiving his degree, he attended the Ecole des Beaux Arts School of Architectural design in Paris, France for his postgraduate education.

He served as the Washington Office architect for the U.S. Forest Service between 1933 and 1953 and provided professional guidance for the service. Groben lived between the years of 1883 and 1961.

Harney/Black Elk Peak Lookout. (Courtesy U.S. Forest Service)

According to the *Deadwood-Pioneer Times* newspaper dated February 17, 1952, the Rankin Ridge Lookout site has been in service since 1952, "A 40-foot cedar pole tower with a crow's nest was moved from Elk Mountain to be used as a temporary lookout." The permanent steel tower pictured above was erected in 1956.

Rankin Ridge Fire Lookout. (Courtesy Dixie Boyle)

The *Deadwood Pioneer Times* also explained the naming of the site in February of 1952, "Rankin Ridge was named for William A. Rankin, first superintendent of Wind Cave National Park. He served in the Spanish/American War with the Rough Riders." Rankin was also part of the group who traveled to Washington, DC and rode their horses in Teddy Roosevelt's inaugural parade.

Rankin Ridge was regularly staffed, being the highest point in Wind Cave National Park, between the years of 1956 and 1998 when the tower was put out of service for safety reasons. The lookout is still occasionally used to check for wildfire as well as to monitor severe weather conditions.

Battle Mountain Fire Lookout was last staffed in the 1990s.
(Courtesy Dixie Boyle)

Rapid City Journal May 1965, "The Game, Fish & Parks Department plans to build a new lookout on Battle Mountain one mile NE of Hot Springs in the southern Black Hills." The lookout was staffed into the 1990s by the South Dakota State Forestry Department. An interpretive sign about the naming of Battle Mountain is interesting. In the 16th Century Native Americans were stricken with an epidemic called "fell disease" that threatened to wipe out the tribe. A messenger arrived with news of the "healing" waters reportedly touched by the finger of the Great Spirit that cured all manner of diseases. The tribes came to the springs by the thousands.

The Cheyenne tribe took possession of the springs in the 1800s and built a tipi city covering hundreds of acres in the area. The Sioux later migrated into the area and disputed ownership of the springs and a battle occurred between the two tribes over possession of the healing waters. The Sioux won the battle and afterwards the mountain was referred to as Battle Mountain. In later years, it became a peaceful location for the tribes to meet where they put their differences aside and got along with one another while using the healing waters.

Homestake Lookout/Observation Deck in Wyoming (Courtesy Dixie Boyle)

In 1922, Homestake Mining Company of Lead, South Dakota utilized a tall, pine tree as a fire lookout. Spikes were driven through the tree and served as a ladder near the bottom. The pine tree was the only lookout used for fourteen years until the Moskee, Buckhorn and Sundance Fires of the 1930s. With the loss of much needed timber, Homestake decided to build a more permanent structure. A steel platform took the place of the pine tree that was eventually used as fire wood at the Moskee Logging Camp. The lookout site initially called the

Moskee Fire Lookout was renamed Homestake Fire Lookout with the construction of the new tower.

There was a need for a fire lookout in the area especially in the 1930s when fires often blew out of control. An article in the *Rapid City Journal* dated November 18, 1976 gives a history of destructive fires throughout the Black Hills in the 1930s and it seems one of the more destructive was the Moskee Fire, "Over 7,000 acres burned in the Black Hills National Forest and timbered land owned by Homestake Mining Company on the edge of the national forest near Moskee, Wyoming. The Moskee Fire was listed as lightning caused but many suspected it had been ignited by an arsonist. Two young men were arrested on suspicion but nothing ever came of it."

Two thousand fire fighters fought the fire at the height of the blaze. The fire could not be brought under control for four days and threatened the lumber camp of Moskee and its 65 residents. Unfortunately, one death occurred when a 22-year-old Civilian Conservation Corps worker from Sioux Falls, South Dakota was struck by a falling pine tree and died in a hospital a short time later.

Moskee Lookout Tree. (Courtesy Doris Vore)

BLACK HILLS FIRE LOOKOUTS
NO LONGER STANDING

Veteran's Peak was established as a secondary lookout in 1939 and only staffed when needed mainly after a lightning storm, when a fire was in progress or during extremely dry weather. The lookout site, located five miles southwest of Sturgis, is now occupied by a radio tower and associated equipment sheds. Nothing remains of the old lookout once found on the peak and much of its history has been lost.

An article in the *Rapid City Journal* dated December 7, 1938 gives a little history of the lookout site, "A secondary lookout is planned for a peak four miles from the Park Creek Veteran's Camp. In recognition of the work done in the northern Black Hills by the veterans at the camp, the new lookout will be named Veteran's Lookout. The tower will be a 30-foot log structure, with a seven-foot square observatory. The peak has been known locally as East Kirk Hill."

Veteran's Peak Fire Lookout. (Courtesy U.S. Forest Service)

Boulder Hill Fire Lookout was built in the spring of 1939 and the tower was staffed until the 1970s. The first person to staff the lookout was William Grover. *Rapid City Journal,* July 22, 1939, "Early this spring a 30-foot tower on Boulder Hill, 5400 feet high, located two miles west of Rockerville was built. Although the lookout is nearly 2000 feet lower than Harney, the lookout was established to spot fires in the extensively used areas south of Rapid, Spring and Battle Creeks."

Boulder Hill was staffed in 1943 by husband-and-wife team, Galin and Effie McCain. Galin was the main fire lookout but Effie was his relief during times of extreme fire danger and they often worked together when the dry months persisted. Effie was a school teacher before marrying Galin and enjoyed the life of a fire lookout.

Boulder Hill Fire Lookout. (Courtesy U.S. Forest Service)

According to an article in the *Rapid City Journal* dated October 16, 1949, Boulder Hill overlooked Rapid City. "Boulder Hill, closest lookout to Rapid City, also has the advantage of spotting a fire within the city limits and notifying the Rapid City Fire Department before it had received a call, almost a metropolitan touch to the mountainous hideaway."

A tornado hit near Boulder Hill in 1966 as described in a July 27 article in the *Rapid City Journal,* "At the halfway point in the storm's path, Boulder Hill Fire Lookout lost some windows and a few boards but was otherwise undamaged. A summer home near Spring Creek lost an outbuilding. The twister hit around 12:30 on Saturday afternoon."

Lakota Peak Lookout Tower (Courtesy South Dakota State Forestry)

The Lakota Peak Lookout is no longer in service and was torn down in the early 2000s. A few old photos remain of the site and one or two articles in newspapers throughout the area. But, overall finding information and history on the lookout is hard to find. Luckily, newspapers in the Black Hills liked to write about their lookout towers and those who staffed them.

Article in *Rapid City Journal* dated June 7, 1961, "Another hermit for hire has taken his place in the second of the state's forestry lookouts. Lawrence Mihills of Custer has moved to a cabin at Lakota Peak northwest of Hermosa to begin his fourth season as a fire lookout. The peak is one of two lookouts maintained by the Game, Fish & Parks Department. The other is on Mt. Coolidge and is operated out of Custer State Park. Mihills set up house-keeping at the cabin Tuesday. He remains on 24-hour call, spending about 10 hours on duty in the tower each day."

A well-written article by Sally Farrar titled: Fire Danger Going up; Lakota Peak Manned in the *Rapid City Journal* dated May 24, 1964 reads, "Fifty Feet Up and Climbing. That's not an airplane but the lookout going to work on Lakota Peak northwest of Hermosa.

With the fire danger rising by the hour, the State Game Fish & Parks Department has swung into action and now posts a lookout atop the peak seven days a week."

The lookout tower was constructed in a joint effort by the Hermosa Volunteer Fire Department, Pennington County & the Game, Fish & Park Department. One of the first primary lookouts at the site was Jim Casselman and his relief Victor Stanley.

The two men worked eight to ten hour shifts and remained at the station to report sleepers and snag fires which come up after lightning storms.

Casselman grew up in Gray's Harbor, Washington. He served in World War II and saw action in Korea. He also staffed lookouts on Boulder Hill and Seth Bullock. In his spare time he worked as a sign writer.

Stanley was raised in North Dakota. He served in the U.S. Air Force for thirteen years before working with the Canadian National Parks. His hobbies included dog training and he took his dog to the lookout after receiving a rattlesnake shot.

The snakebite kit was a necessary piece of equipment atop Lakota Peak. Numerous snakes were killed in previous years near the lookout.

A telephone line was first strung to the site in 1964. Previously, the only contact with the outside world was via radio, hazardous in electrical storms, or a bumpy, rugged ride down the mountain to a nearby ranch house. The lookout was able to contact Rapid City, Piedmont, Ellsworth Air Force Base and other communities. These were all local calls.

It was a lonely job and sometimes a frightening job perched up in the clouds while the wind moves the lookout tower. But it is rewarding in terms of service to fellowman and of the beauty which may be observed from the peak.

In the old cabin once inhabiting the site, a picture window opened over a beautiful landscape. Framed in the middle of the window was an outstanding view of Mount Rushmore.

Visitors were welcome at the former lookout site, but required a pickup or other rugged vehicle to ascend the rough, rugged and rocky terrain to the top.

Pilger Fire Lookout. (Courtesy U.S. Forest Service)

The Pilger Tower was out of service by the 1970s and only the foundations remain. The lookout site is located 22 miles WNW of Hot Springs, South Dakota. According to an article in the *Lead Daily Call* dated November 10, 1976 Willis D. Cloud staffed Pilger Lookout in 1957, "Willis D. Cloud, who went on to make a name for himself as a Black Hills dispatcher started his Forest Service career as a lookout on Pilger Mountain Lookout. In 1957 he began work on both Pilger and Summit Ridge Fire Lookouts."

An article in the *Rapid City Journal* dated January 17, 1963 explains why a lookout site was established at Pilger Lookout, "On the Harney, a new lookout tower was erected on Pilger Mountain to cover a large area on the southwest part of the forest which has been blind to other lookouts in the past. Several fires were seen and reported from this point while construction was in progress."

Parker Peak Fire Lookout. (Courtesy U.S. Forest Service)

Parker Peak Lookout was in service between 1943 and the 1970s and the tower was later dismantled and removed from the site. All that remains are four concrete pads. Doreen Miller was the first lookout assigned to the peak. Gail and Herbert Duncan were long-term lookouts at the lookout site.

According to Gayle Duncan's obituary she was born in September 10, 1919 at Eagle Butte to Fred and Jennie Connell. She married William W. Duncan in the fall of 1938 at Cambridge, Minnesota. She then moved to Hot Springs, South Dakota in 1949 where she operated Gayle's Midget Lunch until the spring of 1952.

She started working for the U.S. Forest Service at Parker Peak in 1952 and remained at the site for six years before moving to Mt. Coolidge in 1958 where she worked the fire tower until the 1970s. In the early 1970s she moved to Custer where she worked in various lookouts including Bear Mountain. She retired in November 1982.

Article in the *Lead Daily Call* dated July 17, 1943: "The Parker Peak forest ranger lookout directly above Minnekahta, was completed July 10, according to announcements by N.E. Hibbard, district forest ranger."

Castle Peak Fire Lookout (Courtesy U.S. Forest Service)

The lookout structure on Castle Peak was torn down in 1961 and the remains scattered over the sides of the summit where the tower once stood. Some sources say it was later burned. Castle Peak was located twenty-five miles west of Rapid City and served as a secondary lookout and only staffed during extreme fire danger. The lookout site was under the administration of the South Dakota State Forestry in conjunction with the Black Hills National Forest.

Castle Peak Fire Lookout, as many in the Black Hills, was placed in service in 1939. Article in *Rapid City Journal* dated October 29, 1939: "A phone line also will be built to Castle Peak. The only communication there is a radio."

Article in the *Lead Daily* newspaper dated October 29, 1977 describes the view from Castle Peak, "Go to Forest Road number 238 which leads to the top of Castle Peak, the site of an abandoned fire lookout. The view from here reaches out into Wyoming to the west and takes in nearly the full scope of the Hills. It is one of the finest vantage points to be found."

June Johnston, Cicero Peak's Last Primary Lookout.
(Courtesy Custer County Chronicle)

June Johnston from Custer, South Dakota was the last person to serve as fire lookout on Cicero Peak. She took her young sons and dogs to the mountaintop each fire season for a decade, reported wildfire, watched weather patterns and enjoyed the solitude of her lookout post. She was heartbroken when her lookout was slated to be removed and the lookout site closed.

Over half of the fire lookouts in the Black Hills National Forest were put out of service in the 1970s when the forest began to lean more toward the use of aerial detection. After Cicero Peak went out of full-time status, it was abandoned on the peak for another seven years and occasionally used to spot forest fires. The lookout was vandalized more than once and even the fire-finder destroyed and thrown down the ridge from where it had been tossed.

When June began her career as a fire lookout, the heyday of staffed fire lookouts in the Black Hills was winding down. Fire management on the forest began to head in a different direction with a push for aerial detection. When June started work in 1964 there were seventeen fire lookouts still in service: Battle Mountain, Parker Peak, Pilger Mountain, Elk Mountain, Summit Ridge, Pisgah Mountain, Warren Peak, Terry Peak, Custer Peak, Bear Mountain, Cicero Peak, Rankin Ridge, Mount Coolidge, Lakota Peak, Harney Peak, Boulder Hill and Flag Mountain. The number of lookouts was narrowed down to six where it has remained for the past half century.

Cicero Peak Fire Lookout. (Courtesy U.S. Forest Service)

June explained how lookout duty has changed yet remained the same over the years, "Bear Mountain and Terry Peak Lookouts were the first to get electricity and were equipped with a base station and electric radios while the rest of us were still on the smaller, battery-operated radio.

It was frustrating at times, because Terry and Bear Mountain Lookouts with the more powerful radios would talk over the rest of us when we were transmitting. The person staffing Terry Peak, not bothering to pay attention to what was going on in the rest of the forest would blow the others off the radio. I was happy when my lookout was wired for electricity, because now I could blow him off the radio.

The lookouts were a close group during these years and when off duty would have gab sessions on the radio at night. June tells of the good-natured competition between the lookout sites, "We were always trying to pick up a smoke in someone else's territory. Bear Mountain would call and ask is that a smoke I see close to your lookout? I would freak out looking for nothing but a little road dust."

One day the shoe was on the other foot when I saw a smoke and called Bear Mountain and asked about the smoke near his tower. He had a fire he had to call in. I smiled. I got him. We were friends but also competitors.

She told another story about the lookout on Parker Peak. Lookouts in the area noticed a large plume of smoke coming up at the Parker Peak Lookout one afternoon and tried calling the lookout station on the radio but no one answered. They were getting concerned when the lookout on duty returned their calls and said their camp stove caught fire in the tower, so they threw it over the ridge. That started a fire which they had to race down and put out.

June pointed out the main responsibility of a fire lookout has always been to locate and report wildfire in an accurate and timely manner. She repeated, this is the lookout's number one duty. As soon as a fire was spotted, we called another lookout with our reading to see if they could give a cross shot for a better location.

During this era in lookout history, lookout stations were placed closer together and they were able to quickly triangulate the fire's location. After a location was determined, the lookout called the forest dispatcher who sent ground crews to the fire, June explained, "Before the use of helicopters, we spent more time leading crews into the fires and relaying on the radio. Another one of our duties was to keep the window glass clean so we could see a fire and to keep the alidade in proper order. The floor had to be clean and shiny at all times in case we had visitors.

After the helicopter came on duty, it was dispatched to the fire if available. Many times, the lookout would call the district fire crew first to give them a head's up and then call in the fire. It was a race to see if the ground crew could beat the helicopter to the fire. The tower was a relay station for radio traffic if needed. We also kept an eye on what the smoke was doing so the crews fighting the fire were informed about the fire's behavior.

One of the first things we did when arriving at the lookout each day was to put up the flag to let the world know we were at the tower. One of the kids was usually in charge of the flag. We always talked to visitors when not busy about the reasons we were staffing the lookout. We were the face of the USFS, so we had to put on a good show.

June explained how lookout duty changed her perspective, "When I first went to the lookout, I used to die for someone to come and see me. By the time I left, I did not want anyone to come and bother me. I enjoyed the heck out of being up watching the world. It was always a new day. We had lightning last night, what is going to happen today? I have to be extra vigilant. Loved watching the bald eagles fly past, the flight of flying ants, the hordes of lady bugs on the rocks below the tower, where else could you get paid to experience such things?"

The original lookout at Cicero Peak was a wooden tower replaced in 1939 with a 30-foot steel tower. The first person to staff the final, steel tower on the peak was Elmer Jorgenson. The lookout had an excellent view of Custer State Park and the Flynn Creek Basin which was a difficult area for the other lookouts to cover. Cicero Peak is named after Cicero James Graham a rancher who once lived at the base of the mountain.

In 1934, Culver, the lookout man on duty at the tower constructed by Camp Mayo of the Civilian Conservation Corps on Cicero Peak, showed marked ability in locating fires before they were large enough to be dangerous. Cicero Peak was an active fire lookout and reported multiple fires in the southern Black Hills area. The lookout being only five miles from Custer was a popular fire lookout. Visitors were often at the site, and the lookout on duty informed them of the fire danger and history of the fire tower. The Black Hills National Forest was proud of their fire lookouts and in newspaper articles they are described as a sharp group of fire lookouts, and the forest praised their abilities.

When Cicero Peak was declared surplus in the 1970s, it was bought by a man from Custer, who in turn sold it to Marine Life in Rapid City in 1980 to serve as a tourist lookout. The lookout exhibit was closed in 1997.

Cicero Peak on its route through Custer to Marine Life in Rapid City.
(Courtesy Custer County Chronicle)

Article in the *Deadwood Pioneer Times* dated July 6, 1953 explains the naming of Flag Mountain Fire Lookout. The article reads, "Probably the only place in the Black Hills where a flag has flown for 75 years on Independence Day is Flag Mountain a 6,900 foot peak west of Deerfield. On July 4, 1876, Joe Reynolds a scout for General Custer placed a flag on the peak as a warning to the surrounding settlers of a threatened Sioux uprising. On each succeeding Fourth of July until his death, he placed a flag on the original site. The custom was carried on by his sons until 1941 when a forest fire lookout was completed. Now the flag flies everyday including July 4 during the fire season."

Flag Mountain Fire Lookout. (Courtesy U.S. Forest Service)

Another article in the Rapid City Journal dated June 27, 1940 tells about the construction at the site. "Construction of three miles of fire road from Reynolds Prairie in the Limestone District of the Black Hills west to Flag Mountain where a fire lookout will soon be built was announced Wednesday by C.C. Averill, Supervisor of the Black Hills National Forest."

August 9, 1946, *The Black Hills Weekly:* "Ranger Dick Howard, Rochford, investigated a smoke reported by Jack Munson, Flag Mountain fire lookout late Tuesday evening, to find out that it was only a bonfire built by summer residents at a cabin, southwest of Rochford to roast wieners for an outdoor picnic.

By fall, the mountain will be marked by a 14 by 14-foot lookout on a 10-foot base. This is the last of the primary lookouts planned for the Black Hills National Forest Averill said. Two more emergency lookouts are planned, one at Crow Peak southwest of Spearfish and at Terry Peak near Lead. A crew of 25 CCC workers from the Black Fox side camp, under the direction of Ray Engleman was building the road to Flag Mountain."

Original Norris Peak Lookout Tree. (Courtesy U.S. Forest Service)

During the early years of the establishment of the U.S. Forest Service, the agency was often under funded. Rangers patrolling the forest for wildfire were expected to provide their own pack string and gear. Lookout trees with platforms secured in the top were often the first fire lookout placed on mountain peaks. Rangers would cut off the top of a tree and construct a primitive platform and stairs leading to the top. The platform was only used before or after a lightning storm of course. Some of the trees were more elaborate than others and were equipped with a railing, chair, telephone, map board and compass. As early as 1905 lookout trees appeared throughout the national forests. Sometimes a cab was built atop one of these platforms or trees before being replaced with a more modern steel tower in later years.

Norris Peak Lookout and Cabin. (Courtesy U.S. Forest Service)

Norris Peak was named after Matt Norris a Black Hills pioneer who moved to the Black Hills by wagon train in 1876 and established his ranch headquarters at the base of Norris Peak. A sub-camp of the CCCs was established near the peak where the crew worked on trail construction, spring development and the building of a shelter cabin for the lookout.

In the 1930s the Black Hills National Forest organized their lookouts as either secondary or emergency and permanent. The emergency lookouts were staffed only during extreme fire danger. One rule the agency put in place for the lookouts was for three days after a lightning storm the lookouts would also be staffed providing lightning had been visible in that area. Norris Peak was an emergency or secondary lookout. Norris Peak Lookout was built in 1938 and disassembled and demolished in 1966.

Article in *Rapid City Journal* dated June 20, 1932: "A 35-foot steel tower on Norris Peak south of Deadwood is ready for a fire lookout, but there is not much for a fire lookout to do this season. Last season a lookout perched in a tall pine tree on Norris Peak to watch for smoke but this season not one fire to date in the Black Hills National Forest it was learned at the headquarters office in Deadwood."

The original wooden lookout tower at the Pisgah Lookout site was erected by members of the CCCs in 1941 under the direction of foreman Leo Harbaugh. The tower was placed on private land owned by Nick Mitich five miles from the Flying V Guest Ranch east of Newcastle, Wyoming.

Construction and maintaining of the lookout tower was a joint endeavor. The first tower was built in 1941 on land obtained through two separate agreements. In 1939 five acres were obtained from the Weston County Commissioners with funds raised by the Newcastle Lion's Club. Five additional acres were obtained in 1943 through a donation from the commissioners of Cambria Park.

In February of 1941 approval was granted to a state WPA Project covering the construction of 15 miles of telephone line from Pisgah Mountain Lookout to Newcastle. The Forest Service furnished the wire, insulators and brackets.

In 1957 a new lookout made of galvanized steel and standing 54 feet high was erected by U.S. Forest Service personnel replacing the original wooden tower on the mountain. The lookout measured 14 by 14 feet and included a living quarters for the person on duty. According to newspaper articles, the lookout was staffed by Mr. and Mrs. W.D. Cloud for 24 hours a day seven days a week.

Original Lookout on Mt. Pisgah in Wyoming.
(Courtesy U.S. Forest Service)

In 1966 the lookout site was considered non-effective and reported few fires, so it was decided to decommission the site. The *News Letter Journal* tells what happened to the lookout in an article dated September 15, 1966, "Construction workers are currently in the process of disassembling the Pisgah Fire Lookout Tower. The tower will be taken to the Seth Bullock lookout site and installed there."

LeNora Sundstrom was possibly the last lookout to staff Mt. Pisgah. According to the Rapid City Journal she staffed the lookout in 1965. Sundstrom enjoyed the experience and was a dedicated fire lookout. She worked each season according to the weather patterns. The year before she came off the tower on November 14 when cold temperatures, snow and fog reduced the fire danger to a minimum.

Mt. Pisgah under Construction showing both the original and second fire lookout. (Courtesy U.S. Forest Service)

Two last U.S. Forest Service Lookout sites are listed in the Black Hills National Forest, Signal Hill and Crow's Nest Peak. Information about Signal Hill was listed in the *Rapid City Journal* in April of 1939, "Signal Hill is located 12 miles W/NW of Custer. There is a 30-foot wooden tower at Signal Hill located in the Limestone Country about three miles NW of Alkali Springs. The station is only staffed during extreme fire danger. No photo was found.

The *Deadwood Daily Pioneer – Times* dated April 29, 1929 tells of the proposed building of Crow's Nest Peak Lookout, "A field tower, for use of rangers in watching for or determining where fires exist, will also be built in the Black Hills National Forest at Crow's Nest. This will be occupied temporarily during the extremely dry season." It is uncertain if this lookout was ever actually erected. It may have been a high point used by fire crews to look for wildfire or an early primitive platform style lookout. No photo has been found.

Another reference to a lookout site named Anchor Hill was found. The lookout was not an official Forest Service Lookout, but a lookout platform built around a live pine tree on land owned by the Anchor Hill Gold Mine near Deadwood. Unfortunately, the wooden platform was lost to fire in 2002 when the Grizzly Fire burned over it.

Reference to a lookout named Piedmont is found throughout newspaper files, but so far no photo or description of the lookout site has been found. It was probably not an official Forest Service Fire Lookout. I found only two hints about the lookout one in the *Daily Deadwood Pioneer-Times* dated August 19, 1928, "Word was received from the lookout station near Piedmont that a fire had broken out." One more hint in the *Black Hills Weekly* dated August 11, 1944, "Emergency lookouts are on duty on Norris Peak, Veteran's Lookout, Piedmont and Anchor Hill."

Anchor Hill Lookout Platform circa 1982
(Courtesy of Anchor Hill Mining Company)

ADDITIONAL FIRE LOOKOUTS IN SOUTH DAKOTA & WYOMING

FIRE LOOKOUTS ON THE PINE RIDGE & ROSEBUD SIOUX INDIANS RESERVATIONS

Two lookouts are listed on the Pine Ridge Sioux Indian Reservation: Eagle Nest and Porcupine Butte: Porcupine Butte – steel tower still standing – It is located midway between Wounded Knee and Porcupine on the Pine Ridge Sioux Indian Reservation.

Through a cooperative agreement between the South Dakota State Forestry, Indian Services and other agencies a steel observation tower was erected on the summit of Porcupine Butte in the 1930s. The tower was used to report prairie fires before they reached Pine Ridge and other communities on the reservation. Medicine Butte Lookout was a cooperative lookout – the cabin disappeared from the peak in 1942. The South Tower Lookout was located on the Rosebud Sioux Indian Reservation but nothing remains at the site.

The *Argus-Leader* dated August 31, 1952 tells of Porcupine Butte, "Porcupine Butte is rich in Native American tradition and lore. From its lofty summit smoke signals often lifted upward into the sky back in the old days, while brave young warriors often watched for signs of the enemy from its high vantage point.

A trail on the south side of the butte branching off from the regular highway, takes you by car to a little cabin formerly used by the lookout during fire seasons, and from here is not so much of a climb to the summit by means of a footpath that weaves and twists upward among the rock ledges and whispering pines."

The *Rapid City Journal* dated August 24, 1939 tells of the building of a fire tower on Porcupine Butte. "The government erected a steel tower, 80 feet high, on the butte in 1937, from which a commanding view may be had of the country for many miles and where a lookout is kept during summer months.

The same article tells of the historical usage of Eagle Nest Butte, Native Americans used Eagle Nest Butte as a medicine place, one of the lofty elevations to which their adolescent youths betook themselves to procure their personal medicines."

FORMER FIRE LOOKOUTS ON SOUTH DAKOTA'S WILDLIFE REFUGES

Scott Lake Fire Lookout (Courtesy Scott Lake Wildlife Refuge)

In addition to the Scott Lake Lookout, another lookout named Sand Lake Lookout is located on the Sand Lake National Wildlife Refuge near Aberdeen. The Sand Lake Observation Tower stands 108 feet high and was built by the CCCs in 1936. The tower is used as a visitor center as well as a location to study large flocks of migrating birds and watch for poachers.

FIRE LOOKOUTS STAFFED IN WYOMING

Five fire lookout stations remain active in Wyoming: Mt. Washburn a part-time, volunteer lookout located in Yellowstone National Park, the Black Mountain Cooperative Lookout staffed through a joint agreement with the USFS, BLM, State Forestry plus Platte, Albany and Converse Counties near Douglas. Blackhall Lookout on the Medicine Bow/Routt has been converted into a rental, but is still used for the detection of forest fires when needed. The history of the remaining two lookouts: Warren Peak and Cement Ridge in the Black Hills National Forest have been previously discussed.

Mt. Washburn Fire Lookout – Staffed by volunteers
in Yellowstone National Park (Courtesy U.S. Park Service)

The first fire lookout appeared on Mt. Washburn in 1921 and by the following year three miles of telephone line had been built from Dunraven Pass to the fire lookout. As early as 1930 the Yellowstone Park Transportation Company had established daily excursions to the top of the mountain. The lookout site was visited by hundreds of tourists each day.

In 1935 Theodore Robb served as a park ranger, naturalist and fire lookout -- a little different job description than for lookouts in the present era. John Mackey from Ansley, Nebraska served as the first lookout at the new lookout tower completed in 1940. He was a student at the University of Nebraska.

One of the first fire lookouts in the Medicine Bow-Routt National Forest was Medicine Bow Peak. The lookout is no longer in service but a Laramie newspaper left behind an interesting concept tried by the forest and lookout on duty. *The Laramie Daily Boomerang* dated September 17, 1911, "Tomorrow a system of smoke signals will be tried on the Medicine Bow National Forest with smoke from the stove atop the Snowy Range. The system is simple, tar covered wood will be burned and the signals will be streams of smoke the number will indicate the location of the fire. The stream of smoke for five seconds will mean Foxpark, two streams of five seconds each with a period of five seconds in between will mean Keystone, and so on."

A small wooden ground cabin was initially built at the site around 1909 and was later replaced with a cupola style lookout.

Black Mountain Cooperative Lookout (Courtesy U.S. Forest Service)

The Black Mountain Cooperative Lookout was built by the U.S. Forest Service in 1958 and is located 26 miles south of Douglas on the Medicine Bow/Routt National Forest.

The Medicine Bow National Forest was established in 1902 and named after the Native American powwows once performed in the area. Different tribes would congregate in the area to search for mountain mahogany, which was an excellent wood the tribes desired to make bows. They also performed rituals hoped to cure diseases and thus make good medicine.

In 1995 the Medicine Bow National Forest, Routt National Forest and Thunder Basin National Grasslands were combined due to the budget and their close proximity to one another. The Routt National Forest was established in 1905 and named after John Routt the first governor of Colorado. The Thunder Basin National Grasslands is mainly leased to cattle ranchers. The area is wide open country with distinct landmarks in all directions. The Cheyenne tribe stacked rocks throughout the grasslands in order to find their way when passing through the area. Many of the rock piles remain as evidence of their former occupation.

LOOKOUT RENTALS IN WYOMING

Lookout rentals are between $40 and $80 a night and early reservations are recommended.

Blackhall Mountain, located in Wyoming's Sierra Madre Range in the south-central section of the state is at the end of one of Wyoming's highest roads. The lookout was built in 1963. Used for twenty years and then put on standby as needed status. Renovated and now used as a rental as well as a fire tower during extreme conditions. Spruce Mountain is also a popular rental.

Sheep Mountain Fire Lookout Rental Site (Courtesy U.S. Forest Service)

Sheep Mountain Lookout was built in 1950 and closed in the 1970s. The lookout is located 18 miles SW of Buffalo. The lookout was converted into a rental and the site is open weather permitting between the months of June and October. The Lookout Rental Program has become popular throughout the nation and visitors enjoy spending a few days or weeks vacationing at a former lookout station.

3
LOOKOUTS ONCE LOCATED IN THE PLAINS STATES

In an era before Texas and other Plains States began to use aerial observers, the state staffed over a hundred fire lookout stations. In the 1960s, the Texas Forest Service began to put many of their fire towers out of service and they were sold or moved from their original locations. None of the Texas fire towers remain in service but several remain standing.

The fire lookout structures throughout the Plains states were mainly Aermotors rising between 90 and 125 feet high. Most of these lookout stations could see between twenty and thirty miles on a clear day. Aermotor was a company in Chicago that constructed windmills and lookout towers. Thirty foot towers would not work in Texas due to the flatness of the land, the higher the towers the better the view.

The *Alto Herald* dated April 12, 1928 tells of early cooperation between agencies in fighting and reporting wildfire, "The Texas Forest Service in cooperation with the Southern Pine Lumber Company and the Houston County Timber Company has just completed the erection of two towers for forest fire detection purposes.

Each tower is 90 feet in height equipped with ladders and landing platforms and surmounted with a glass enclosed cab 8 ½ feet square. One tower is located at Ratcliff in eastern Houston County and the other on Bird Mountain in southeastern Anderson County."

Newspapers in Texas provide some interesting information about the Love's Lookout Tower in the *Tyler-Morning Telegraph* dated June 11, 1936, "A state forestry tower at Love's Lookout State Park has been completed and will be placed into use immediately."

Another article in the same newspaper dated October 15, 1936 explains the popularity of the lookout site, "Hundreds of visitors are being attracted to a new Texas Forest Service fire lookout tower located on the highest portion of Love's Lookout State Park near Jacksonville. From its view of the East Texas countryside for a distance of some 30 to 35 miles may be obtained. In 31 days, a total of 1380 registered visitors braved the dizzying heights of the 100 foot climb to have a better view of the beauty from the lookout."

Around 1910, the bluff where the fire tower still stands was named after an early pioneer named Wesley Love. He settled in the area in 1904 and bought much of the land surrounding the lookout site and planted a 600-acre peach orchard.

President Franklin D. Roosevelt's Works Progress Administration (WPA) built a park on Love's land in the 1930s with a popular picnic area, a swimming pool, dance pavilion and location for sunrise services, plays and other community events. During its heyday, people drove from as far away as Dallas and Houston to enjoy a weekend picnic.

Chandler Fire Lookout is one of a few lookouts in Texas that remain standing. (Courtesy Texas State Forestry)

Another interesting article was found in the *Gilmer-Mirror* dated December 1, 1960, "A forest fire lookout has been erected on Chamberlain Mountain in the Latch area in southwest Upshur County.

Located on O.V. Schuler land, the tower is primarily to be used to help another tower at Pine Mills pinpoint fire sites in Wood County. A large area of Wood County adjoining Upshur County is a newly formed fire protection district. An oil company and paper company helped start the fire district with contributed funds."

The Scott Tower on the Bessie Ranger District in Nebraska's Halsey National Forest was severely damaged in the Bovee Fire of 2022. The fast moving fire burned over the popular lookout site and 4-H Campground nearby. After inspection of the lookout structure, the Bessie Ranger District has been given approval to rebuild the stairs and platform at the lookout site and hope to have it ready for the 2025 fire season.

From the beginning of its history, the Scott Tower was a popular tourist attraction and destination point. As early as the 1950s, over three thousand visitors registered at the tower. People from thirty-two states and six foreign countries visited the tower in 1966. The lookout site serves as both a visitor center and fire lookout.

The Scott Tower was staffed mainly after lightning storms and during high fire danger and was open for afternoon tours for those visiting the site. Before the Bovee Fire, the U.S. Forest Service offered nursery and lookout tours, nature walks and wildflower excursions.

The Bessey Ranger District was named after a pioneer botanist named Charles Bessey. He was the first to believe it was possible to grow a forest of trees in the middle of the sandhills. Many thought he was crazy and his idea was not popular in the beginning. The area had always been cattle country and no one saw a reason to change it.

Bessey was determined to try his experiment and convinced President Teddy Roosevelt to set aside two large tracts as forest reserves in the middle of the sandhills in 1902. He was also able to convince the federal division of Forestry to set up a small plantation west of Swan in Holt County.

The Scott Lookout Tower was named after Charles Scott who was instrumental in the creation of the Halsey National Forest. He was in charge of tree planting between 1902 and 1907. To the surprise of many, the trees did grow and decades later the forest boasted 20,000 acres of trees and was touted as the largest hand planted forest in the United States. Unfortunately, the Bovee Fire destroyed the trees as well.

There were six other fire towers or lookout points scattered throughout the Nebraska National Forest. Many of the lookouts had unusual names and did not seem to remain in service for long. The lookouts were named: the Winnebago Lookout, Eagle Point Lookout, Crescent Lake North Lookout, Crescent Lake South Lookout, Valentine NWR#1 and Valentine NWR#2.

An interesting article was published in the *Walthill Citizen* newspaper in December of 1940 about the Winnebago Lookout Tower. Unfortunately the article did not list the author.

"On one calm and balmy Indian summer day just recently past, we followed the road that winds through the neat buildings of the Winnebago Agency and climbs over a long grade gradually into the hills. We turned sharply and followed a trail that was steeper and narrower, so narrow, in fact the over-hanging branches of the trees seemed to grab like a mischievous child leaving trailing finger marks along the car side. Finally, we came to the crest and here it was the lookout tower.

A steel tower with winding stairs was easy to climb for the most daring souls. Those of our party who had the strength and courage to climb to the top were rewarded with a wonderful view of the river, trees and sky.

A few years ago they tell us, the government built this tower and employed for a brief space of time a forest lookout to be on hand in case of forest fires. The attendant had a house too and further down the hill toward the river we discovered the remains of what had once been a darling little house built of stained logs, the interior now sadly gutted."

Leland Decona, a 31 year old member of the Winnebago tribe was the first lookout to staff the site. His main duties were looking for wildfire as well as illegal wood cutters in the area. The lookout had an amazing view to the north of Big Bear Hollow, River's End, Robber's Cave in the rock cliffs and Blackbird Hill on the Omaha Reservation. To the east across the river in Iowa the towns of Saliz, Sloan and Onawa sparkled in the sun on a clear day.

The Scott Lookout Tower after it burned. (Courtesy U.S. Forest Service)

Iowa had only one fire tower throughout its history the Yellow River Fire Lookout. The steel tower was acquired from the U.S. Forest Service in the 1950s and rebuilt in 1962 on the Yellow River State Forest by the Iowa Department of Natural Resources.

An article in the *Ames Daily Tribune* dated July 6, 1963 tells of the lookout, "The closest thing to an Iowa wilderness will be officially opened to campers this year and named the Yellow River Forest located near Harper's Ferry in northeast Iowa. The first fire lookout in Iowa offers interesting sidelights to the natural attractions in the area. From the top of the recently completed fire tower you can see more than 20 miles on a clear day. "

In the 1930s, the area that would become the Yellow River State Forest had been severely cut over by wood cutters and the state purchased tracts of land and planted thousands of pine trees in what became known as the Paint Creek Experimental Forest. The forest has flourished and become a major recreation area for camping and hiking.

The lookout remains standing but is no longer staffed and visitors are not allowed to climb the tower. The lookout was placed on the National Historical Lookout Register in 1995 and the National Register of Historic Places in 2021.

The tower was often described in newspaper articles as being obsolete even before it was built, as this was an era when many fire lookouts were put out of service throughout the country. It never played a major role in fire suppression.

Yellow River Fire Lookout near McGregor, Iowa
(Courtesy U.S. Forest Service)

4
THREE FORMER LOOKOUTS IN CALIFORNIA

Little Mount Hoffman Fire Lookout in the Shasta National Forest in 1952
(Courtesy author's collection)

How many times have you found an old photograph and wondered about the identities of the people pictured? Wondered what year the photo was taken and what event the group was attending? But, there was no identification or dates on the photograph. Of course the information can still be tracked down, but it will take a lot more digging.

It is important to label the old photographs you have in your possession. When it comes to lookout photos be sure and include the name of the lookout site, year photo was taken and who was staffing the lookout at the time of the picture. If no information is left on the photo there is a good chance the history could be lost.

Over a decade ago, a friend gave me three, old photos of lookout sites in California where he had worked when he was younger. They seemed such magical sites, and I often wondered about their pasts. This winter while snowed in a few days, I once again took out the old photos to see what I could find about their past history.

These lookouts were unfamiliar to me, but I was able to discover many interesting facts about them because the person taking the picture had labeled them with only two facts: name of lookout and date. I found all three lookouts have been out of service since the 1970s and except for California's Little Mount Hoffman have been removed from their mountain peaks.

Little Mount Hoffman also went out of service for the detection of forest fires in the 1970s but was still used to occasionally locate a fire. Fortunately, the lookout was restored in 1994 and in 1998 converted into a popular rental already booked a year ahead. Visitors can stay at the historic lookout for $75.00 a night.

Little Mount Hoffman sits on the edge of Medicine Lake Highland, the largest identified volcano in California. The site at 7309 feet provides one of the best views of the surrounding area as well as of Mt. Shasta and Mt. Lassen.

Grizzly Peak Fire Lookout in 1952 (Courtesy author's collection)

The second photo is of Grizzly Peak erected on the McCloud Ranger District circa 1913. According to newspaper articles, in that year the Shasta National Forest transported lumber and supplies to Grizzly Peak with plans to erect a fire lookout. It seems a primitive lookout was built at that time.

The lookout structure in the photo was built in 1923 but replaced with a five foot block tower in 1963. The block tower was airlifted by helicopter in 1975 to Hogback Mountain above the Pitt River. It served as the Hogback Mountain Lookout for thirty seven years until it was severely vandalized and removed from the peak in 2012.

Bob Gray staffed the lookout site in 1942 and his cousin Pearl Cowan worked the lookout in the 1950s. Gray went on to become a full-time employee with the U.S. Forest Service as a fire crew foreman and dispatcher.

Only portions of a rock wall are found at Black Butte Fire Lookout, and nothing remains of the three different lookouts used during different eras at the site. The first lookout and trail to access the lookout were built by the Civilian Conservation Corps in the late 1930s. The lookout was destroyed by the Columbus Day Storm of 1962 and rebuilt the following year.

Black Butte Fire Lookout in 1952 (Courtesy author's collection)

The lookout was demolished in the strong winds of the storm. The roof was completely blown off, most of the catwalk blew away, one wall had caved in, there was glass everywhere and the fire finder was covered in snow. A second lookout was erected on the butte in 1963 and served as the lookout for the next fifteen years until it was relocated to Hogback Mountain in 1978.

Painting of Grizzly Peak Lookout by Bob Gray, former lookout and author of the book *Forests, Fires & Wild Things* (Courtesy author's collection)

CONCLUSION

The majority of the American public would have little desire to spend every summer alone on an isolated mountain peak with few conveniences and report forest fires. Many would not enjoy the small space of the lookout tower with only wildlife, sunsets, wind and their dog for company. Yet, the job suits a small percentage of the population that return to lookout jobs throughout the country each fire season. It definitely takes a certain breed to spend months alone with little human contact.

The first lookout personnel often helped to build the towers they staffed. Supplies were packed in by mule train and expected to last half of the season before another load arrived. The early lookouts had to be self-sufficient and be able to protect themselves from wild animals and accidents. They did not see another person for months at a time and were expected to haul their own water, chop their own wood and repair phone lines when communication was down. These lookouts were true pioneers and paved the way for future lookouts in the field.

On the other hand, there were those who lasted only a day, week or month before realizing the isolation and solitude of lookout duty did not appeal to them. One volunteer left his lookout post one afternoon on Cement Ridge and packed up and left without informing his supervisor and was never heard from again.

Another lookout staffed a tower for three weeks before reporting he saw aliens land near his lookout tower. He too gave up on lookout duty and returned to a job in the city. One lookout quit after seeing her first rattlesnake and another after reporting the moon as a massive wildfire late one night. But, the majority of those who staff lookouts year after year do not mind the isolation and that is the main reason they take a job as a fire lookout.

The life of a fire lookout is often described as romantic, and this is true most of the time especially on full-moon nights and during morning sunrises. But, there is a day to day grind to the job especially during the "dog days of summer" when one day seems the same as the one before. There are days when the flying ants and moths are relentless. When the temperature along the Rio Grande Valley reaches triple digits and there is no breeze to stir the sultry air or clouds to provide shade,

But, lookout life is more than rewarding, and there's a certain satisfaction in pinpointing a fire before anyone else sees it and helping crews to find its location before it spreads and becomes a bigger problem. There's also a feeling of self-sufficiently in living alone all week and interacting with nature as the first pioneers did in the past.

The remaining five hundred or so fire towers still in service throughout the country continue to report forest fires each year. Some members of the American population do not believe fire towers are still staffed while others think it is time for them to be permanently retired in favor of modern technology. The future of fire lookouts is uncertain but for now they continue in service throughout our nation's forests and are an integral part of fire programs.

The Forest Fire Lookout Association (FFLA) has documented most of the lookout sites throughout the country. The organization has developed the National Historic Lookout Register which lists both present and past lookout sites. Photos and historical information can be found on the register plus ownership and date lookouts were built and also removed from their mountain peaks. If you know of a lookout that is not on one of these lists please fill out information to have it listed.

Original Medicine Bow Fire Lookout in Wyoming
(Courtesy U.S. Forest Service)

REFERENCES

Scott, Sylar S. *The National Register of Historic Places Evaluation of Administrative Structures on the Black Hills National Forest, South Dakota and Wyoming.* Vol. 1 October 1988

English, Jane and Eddy, Bonnie. *Mount Shasta's Black Butte: Stories, History, Art, Geology, Photographs.* Mount Shasta, California: Earth Heart Publishing, 2002.

Gray, Bob. *Forests, Fires and Wild Things.* Happy Camp, California: Naturegraph Publishers, Inc., 1985.

Lookouts of the Southwestern Region. Cultural Resources Management Report No. 8 USDA Forest Service. Southwestern Region, September 1989.

Custer History to 1976. Custer County Historical Society. Rapid City, South Dakota. Dakota: Printing Incorporated 1977.

Pioneers of Crook County 1876 to 1920. Crook County Historical Society, Crook County, Wyoming. Pierre, South Dakota: State Publishing Company, 1981.

Personal interview with Bob Sullivan, 6/1993

Personal phone interview with Ed Mason, 6/1996

Personal interview with Lester Mauch, 7/1990

Personal interview with Kenny Sallee, 8/1993

Personal interview with Earl Hamilton, 6/1993

Personal interview with June Johnston, 11/2024

Personal interview with Karen Maloy, 12/2024

National Historic Lookout Register – online

Rex's Fire Lookout Page – online

Newspapers.com – Online – Newspapers used listed in body of manuscript

Zinn, Barb. *Fire Lookout History of the Santa Fe National Forest,* 2017

Oso Ridge Fire Lookout in New Mexico's Zuni Mountains
(Courtesy author's collection)

Author with her lookout partner Maggie at Capilla Peak Fire Lookout
(Courtesy Marilyn Conway)

AUTHOR BIOGRAPHY

Dixie Boyle has worked as a fire lookout for thirty-seven years and could not imagine any other career. She began working as a lookout in New Mexico's Gila and Cibola National Forests and went on to work for the Oregon State Forestry near John Day and in the Black Hills of Wyoming and South Dakota.

In addition to her lookout experience, Dixie worked as a high school history teacher for twenty years before retiring early and taking a full-time lookout position. She was also a newspaper reporter, museum curator, park guide, living history performer and freelance writer.

Dixie has written numerous books and articles on local history. She was awarded a Heritage Preservation Award from the state of New Mexico in 2017 for her book: *A History of Highway 60 and the Railroad Towns on the Belen, New Mexico Cutoff,* as well as her grass roots approach to preservation.